Think *before*
You Think

A Playbook for Mastering Life

Vikki Ann Bless

BALBOA.
PRESS

A DIVISION OF HAY HOUSE

Balboa Press books may be ordered through booksellers or by contacting:

Balboa Press
A Division of Hay House
1663 Liberty Drive
Bloomington, IN 47403
www.balboapress.com.au
1 (877) 407-4847

Because of the dynamic nature of the Internet, any web addresses or links contained in this book may have changed since publication and may no longer be valid. The views expressed in this work are solely those of the author and do not necessarily reflect the views of the publisher, and the publisher hereby disclaims any responsibility for them.

The author of this book does not dispense medical advice or prescribe the use of any technique as a form of treatment for physical, emotional, or medical problems without the advice of a physician, either directly or indirectly. The intent of the author is only to offer information of a general nature to help you in your quest for emotional and spiritual well-being. In the event you use any of the information in this book for yourself, which is your constitutional right, the author and the publisher assume no responsibility for your actions.

Any people depicted in stock imagery provided by Thinkstock are models, and such images are being used for illustrative purposes only.
Certain stock imagery © Thinkstock.

Print information available on the last page.

ISBN: 978-1-5043-0576-1 (sc)
ISBN: 978-1-5043-0577-8 (e)

Balboa Press rev. date: 12/06/2016

Contents

Acknowledgements

With Grace

To all of my family and friends, thank you for your unconditional love and support. There are too many of you to mention, just know you all touch my heart in your own special way.

And Gratitude

To everyone that I ever have crossed paths with throughout my life, thank you for the impact you had on me, although I may not have been able to appreciate it at the time. Some of my greatest realizations have come from my biggest challenges. Even when I did not think I could take away anything of value from them then, I certainly have now.

Dedicated To

My greatest achievement, my son Mitchell, for having such wisdom and clarity beyond your years. You have dealt with many difficult situations early in your life with such maturity and acceptance. For that, and many more reasons, you make me very proud. I understand now that the bond I recognized when I first held you was not just that of a mother and son, but one that spans many lifetimes before. I love you.

And The Departed

To all my departed loved ones, especially Mum and Dad, my sister Gayle, and my little mate Cooper. Thank you for your guidance. I feel you with me every step of the way and I know you will always be watching over all of us. Until we meet again. . . .

Introduction

Have you ever had a thought that was realized? Were you so blown away when it materialized into your life? Have you ever had a thought about someone else and within a split second they called or you ran into them that day? Do not dismiss these seemingly coincidental events. Your mind is so much more powerful than you give it credit for. You have thousands upon thousands of thoughts each day and every single one of them counts. Your thoughts make up all that you have ever been and all that you are going to be. Start making them all count. Start to make them work for you.

1

Something to Think About

Welcome to this book. You would not have been attracted to this book if you did not have a desire for a better life and a need to know how to implement some valuable information for improving your circumstances. I can assure you that you've come to the right place. It is no accident you are here. Your wanting for more is what brought you not only to this juncture in your life, but also to these pages. *Like attracts like.* You wanted an answer to something, and this book has appeared. It is not by coincidence. Some of your questions have been asked millions of times before you by many, many people, however, the way the question has been asked is the way the answer has been given. Meaning, not all questions are asked the same way, so the answers would also greatly differ. Many did not have a strong enough urge to do anything about it or did not believe they would find an answer, even though there was one. However, some people's desire was much stronger than others, and the more questions asked has given those prepared to receive more clarity in gaining an answer.

The intention of this book is to improve your life simply by changing your thoughts. It is a little hard to imagine that our thoughts could be holding us back, but I am here to tell you that if you knew how powerful your thoughts are, you will really start to *Think Before You Think*. If you had any idea how your negative thoughts get in the way of you having your desires met, surely you would want to know. Change your life purely by changing the way you think? Yes, it really is as simple as that. Your life will improve dramatically once you start understanding some basic principles and implementing these new strategies. You may be thinking, *'How can this be? How can I be my thoughts?'*

It is understandable to only believe what it is you can see, what is tangible, to look at your everyday circumstance and what is currently present in your life, instead of having faith that you actually create your

3

world with your thoughts and then see it materialize down the track. If this information had been presented to me years ago I would never for a moment have considered the truth behind it, so your apprehension is expected. However, this kind of thinking will never improve your circumstance beyond what you can see. If you can keep an open mind, and spend some time observing, you will come to see the new reality this book can help you create.

Have a productive thought. You will
be thankful in the long run.

Think Before You Think has been written so you can stop wondering why you have not gotten everything that you have dreamed of. It will show you how to implement the simple techniques to make thinking work for you and what thoughts are holding you back. Many will tell you that you need to provide something in return for your desires; however, based on my own experiences, I do not believe that to be 100 percent correct. What I have noticed is that when you do with the intention of assisting others, an undeniable force yields to you in raising your level of vibration, bringing about desires faster. Many people do like to be of service, and my belief is that this will advance your spiritual development.

I do suggest you read each section in the book even if it is not an area of concern for yourself, as most of the principles and thought processes apply to all situations. I also did not want to repeat information in each chapter that is applicable to other issues as well. There are also stories throughout that relate to not just the chapter it has been assigned and is useful to apply to other areas. If what you read is of little value to you, you may be able to help someone else who is having difficulty with that aspect of their life. So please, don't skip any of it. I recommend you use a highlighter to mark parts of the book that you feel resonate strongly within you. It will make it easier for you to refer back to them at another time. There is also pages at the back of the book for taking notes or writing down any of your own inspirations that may come to you while reading.

There will be concepts expressed throughout *Think Before You Think* that you may have difficulty in comprehending. That's okay and is to be expected, I did not come to these conclusions overnight and would not expect you to either. If this is the case, simply dismiss them. Do not try and convince yourself of anything until you start seeing some proof and can get to a place where you can accept them. In time, it may become a possibility for you, and it may not. Do not focus on anything you find too unbelievable, just try to be open to the information being delivered.

These words have not been written with the intention of spiritually enlightening you, although some may find glimpses of inspiration between the cover. This book has not been written with the intention of making you rich, although of course you can you the principles to help improve your financial situation. The purpose of these words are to help you gain more control of your life, to eliminate many of those unwanted little annoyances (and maybe some big ones) that take up so much of your time. Time that could be better spent doing what is most important to you. The second aim is to help you to alleviate any fear, guilt, worry and frustration that your daily circumstances are causing you.

Think Before You Think is a culmination of what I have learnt, studied, observed, and experienced throughout my life so you may have an easier path. A path that took me years and years to figure out. Some never get to experience this happiness or ease of lifestyle because they do not believe or have a strong desire to find an easier path in their life. Some are so frustrated with their life they have no idea where to start. Many have been ingrained with the idea that life was meant to be difficult and that we should all struggle. They think taking an easier path is cheating, so they won't wish to change their mindset. Obviously you do. I hope you enjoy this book as much as I have in bringing this material to you.

Clarification

Before you continue reading, I wish to clarify the meaning of a few words used throughout the book, these being *'bad'*, *'wrong'* and *'mistake'*. The reason for this is because I don't believe there are such things as these, only experiences that you may no longer wish to repeat. Everything in life is a learning curve. If you look at it that way, it will help to relieve any guilt surrounding the experience. One example is, if I say you are in a *'bad'* or *'wrong'* situation that you believe was a *'mistake'*. Whatever the issue was, it helped you to have an experience that will benefit you, whether you enjoyed it or not. What I am trying to convey is that although certain situations may not to your liking; there is not a *'bad'* or *'wrong'* situation, as anything in your life gives you the opportunity for extra growth and understanding.

Another clarification I want to make is the use of the word *'universe'*. When referring to this word it will be used in the context of which you may choose to define God, Spirit, Allah, Angels, Divine Intelligence or any other interpretation you may have for such 'Higher Power'.

3

Understanding How Powerful Your Thoughts Are

I was a very big believer that things happened for a reason, and stuff happened that was beyond your control, that you really needed to learn how to deal with that which was dished out to you. Now that has all changed. Yes, you do have to deal with the hiccups that come your way to the best of your ability; but once you start to think differently, these difficulties will be few and far between. I have come to realize that we actually put almost everything in our lives ourselves, and the universe just happens to then deliver in a way that we do not think could be possible, that something greater than us made it happen. Well yes, it did; the universe listened and then responded by delivering to you, as it does always. We are the creator of our lives so learn to create effectively.

Saying it was by accident that I stumbled across this information is not true, for there is no such things as accidents, and my beliefs about that have since changed. Luck had nothing to do with it either. Everyone creates his or her own luck. We put it all there ourselves; we just do not realize it. However, I was not aware of this at the time, and I myself was looking for something more. I had a desire for more. How do I make my life easier? What is life all about? What is the purpose of it all? How do I live my desires instead of life living me? I wondered why some people succeeded, while others didn't, even though they were so similar in many ways such as their upbringing and intelligence.

To have some sort of spiritual base or at least an open mind to be able to be receptive to this material helps, as something bigger than what we can see with the naked eye is at work here. Something out there is dancing with us; we have simply been oblivious to it. However, you do not need to believe in anything or even understand it for it to be working for you, as it is working all the time, whether you believe in it or not. You cannot switch it off. I am going to use the words *vibration, frequency,* and *energy* many times throughout this book even when it is hard to comprehend. That is because all things are on some sort of wavelength that we can't witness, but we know it is out there.

Take our computers for instance. We turn on the button yet we really do not understand how they work. We can somehow type a few words in an email and within seconds it could be halfway across the world. Now, we know that even a plane ride to that destination, the fastest mode of transport, would take twenty hours to physically get there. Yet in a matter of seconds we have managed to communicate with someone thousands and thousands of miles away. We don't doubt or question it. We don't need to understand how it works; we just take it for granted that it does and trust every time we wish to communicate via that method. The same goes for your car, microwave, mobile phone, and many other gadgets we take for granted day in, day out; it is the same with the principles of the universe. You don't have to know how it works for it to be happening, but it is to your benefit to work out the basic techniques so you can use it to your advantage.

You get what you think, hence the law of attraction. It may not happen instantaneously, and there is good reason for that. Use it wisely. Use it to your advantage. Everything is energy. The problem is we don't see it, so we don't believe it. We think we are just physical beings in a physical body, but we are so much more than that.

Before I tell you how I came about this information and this book, I will be sharing with you pieces of my life and beliefs that got me to this point as well as personal stories that I am sure you will be able to relate to. Whatever references I make on a spiritual basis, religious or otherwise, this is my experience. Anyone who does not share my beliefs is by no means exempt from this material because it does not take a spiritual or religious outlook for it to work for you. I realize now it was working for me all the time before I had my life-altering experiences.

The reason for my stories is to impress upon you that if someone who had been as skeptical as I can alter and reverse their beliefs, then the most oppressed of people can turn their lives around if they so choose.

The Journey

This search was more than likely brought on after a few incidents that happened in my thirty-fourth year and the following. I was simply stumbling and fumbling through life. I really had no spiritual basis at all before this age, except for the belief that this was not the only chance at life we get, as to me it didn't make any sense that if the world kept on existing, why didn't we? I was the most practical and matter-of-fact person I knew. If we went to sleep at night and woke up with no recollection, wasn't it logical that would happen each time we died? Didn't we just sleep a while when we died and then wake up in a new body? This to me, made perfect sense. Other than that, I had no belief in God or things happening for a reason, because if there was a God, why would so many bad things happen to good people and not the bad people of the world?

I remember one Sunday when I was about four years of age, my mother sent me to Sunday school against my wishes. I protested the whole time I was there and made it known I would never go back. Even back then, at that tender age, I thought that if there was a God, then why did we never have enough money, and I saw what a struggle life was from early on. I felt even at that young age people were judging us. Surely if there was a God, he would not leave three children aged one, four, and five at home alone in the morning because both parents had to slave away at menial jobs to keep the rent paid and food in our mouths.

Life seemed difficult and like a lot of hard work, and I often wondered what the bother was all about? I got the distinct impression that everyone was out to fend for themselves, no one could be trusted and everyone was out to get you, to beat you down. From what I observed for as long as I can remember, the people who got the most respect were the ones that had money and were good at everything, so most of my life was focused on winning at all costs and accumulating riches. In my thirty-fourth year that all changed. I had some very personal experiences that led me on a search.

All of my life until recently, I felt that seeing was believing. If you could not see it, to me it didn't exist. I was quite the pessimist in almost every area of life. Something had to proved to me before I would consider it viable. I remember my sister telling me a story of a motorbike accident she had as a teenager where she nearly died. She told me that when she was in hospital, she was on the ceiling looking down at herself, and all the doctors and nurses were around her body where some of her internal organs were lying open on the table. I thought she had gone crazy. I was a very rational person and certainly wouldn't put up with any kind of nonsense way of thinking.

There came a time in my life, not long after this incident and many years of analyzing, when I realized that there must be some sort of God or at least a bigger picture for all this to be happening in the first place. There must be a reason why tragedy befalls some families and not others. If there was a God, did he love some families more than others? On the surface, this is exactly why people come to think like this however, I knew this thought just didn't make sense. Did some of us come here for the struggle and others not? If so, I never understood why. What is the purpose of existing and struggle, to life in general? I figured there must be a master plan; I simply didn't know what it was.

Up until this age in my life, things were okay but there had to be more. I was fed up with the daily grind, and life just seemed like work; cleaning, running around, paying bills, and struggling to get ahead. By the time all that was done it was time to do it all over again. I was sick of the constant push and pull. Trolley wars in the supermarket, road rage on the streets, rushing from one place to the next, being at work and dealing with difficult people, dealing with difficult people everywhere, worrying if I was safe, if my son was safe, if he was coping at school. Life seemed like a constant barrage of worry and stress, and I had had enough, yet I was only in my thirties. Surely, I can't just be doing this until the day I die?

However, the main issue surrounding this time and the next few years of my life was, that for the first time, things that I had really, really wanted started to elude me. I got to a point where most of my life at this stage was not turning out as I had hoped. The worst part was I couldn't understand why. I just could not put my finger on it. Most of my life I did get what it was I wanted, so why not now? Especially since I was applying so much more physical effort than ever before. Sure, some of my goals weren't that high; however, I almost always got what I wanted, and when I look back at the past, I got way more than I ever thought I had. *So why not now?*

It took me a while before I found the answer, but once I started to ask the right questions and be clearer with my asking, the right answers eventually came. In fact, they pretty much fell into my lap as that is how the laws of the universe work. You simply have to ask, and be receptive to the answer. And it took me all that time to work out that the reason I was not getting what it was I desired, was that I was trying too hard to make things happen. Anything you desire should come to you without being constant battle.

I became aware that my thoughts were not as productive as they had been in the past, which in turn prevented my desires from eventuating. During this time, I went through my share of difficulties which included a divorce, the death of my sister, my mother very ill in hospital, and a heartbreak I had great difficulty in trying to shake. My life felt more like a chore and I was struggling to find any reason to want to breathe. Because of this I was finding it quite arduous to focus on anything worthwhile; it took me a while to realize that unless I did, nothing was going to change. The hardship lead me to a working environment of others who had been toughened by life, but not yet understanding these universal laws, I had not at this point made any connection, that my dismay was attracting more of the same.

What you are thinking now will manifest in the future.
Are you happy with your current thought?

The difficulties I brought upon myself, that had not occurred to me that I created, led me to wanting an easier life and answers on the subject started to come to me. I still at this point had not put two and two together until years later, and I was constantly questioning, *Can you really get what you think about?* Does it really work that way? I began to access my past and that of others, and the light switch finally flicked on. I gave much thought to my former years and to my astonishment, many things I had simply thought of, both good and bad, had materialized without me having to apply any action whatsoever. Whether it was an event, person, object, or circumstance, my thought became my reality.

Before this revelation I turned to spirituality to find answers to my questions; however, even though it offered some comfort, it far from alleviated my emotional pain. I went through a period in my life when things were not working out for me; I was frustrated to say the least. Most things had always worked out for me, and now I was entering a period where there seemed to be quite a lull. Now, after years of searching, I believe I have not only found some peace but the answer to one of life's biggest mysteries. What I found was really quite unbelievable, especially to a real non-believer. I realized I had come across a pattern.

The clincher came for me when I worked a short stint in real estate. Being a rookie, I had no idea how I would be successful; however, I was excited by my new career choice and somehow knew it I would fumble my way through it. My aspirations were high and nothing was going to deter me from achieving them. I had great success in my new occupation from the moment I started, more so than some of the most experienced agents, so I knew the answer had nothing to do with experience. But as the months passed, I wasn't enjoying the line of work I had entered into; and my mixed feelings started to bring mixed results, again not being aware of this at the time. I started to feel resentful at this point, having made yet another career change that I found unfulfilling. I thought I would just have to work harder and longer, push my way through it to improve my results, but to no avail. So how could I be working harder than ever and not be achieving the same level of results?

Not only that, but I recognized for whom I was selling on behalf of had a huge influence on whether their property would sell quickly and for a good price, and it was based on their thought processes. Those who thought a move would be good but were happy whether they sold or not got the best results quickly, and those who put up resistance and worried about the outcome didn't. One couple told me they did not think their property would sell and six months later, their home was still on the market. Another was going through a financial crisis and not until she stopped fighting it did her property sell. Another client, after four months on the market when everything else sold in the first week due to the boom, told me in the latter stages that nothing ever worked out for them and bingo, that's exactly what they got! Another took a little while, but eventually sold once the right home for them came along. What I realized was that all these problem properties came in the time when I was thinking I had made the wrong career choice, so I had actually attracted these clients to me. In the beginning, when I was excited with my new career, I attracted homes that would move fast, ones that I was attuned to.

While I was at this job I had little time to maintain my home due to my work hours, especially the gardens, and had a fleeting thought of who I would get to do these chores for me. I was not too concerned and knew I would work it out and everything would be fine. That night, my brother-in-law, who is a fantastic handyman, said he was working in Sydney and asked if he could stay with me and in return he would maintain my property. My logical thinking started to go out the window, as I had now found enough proof to justify to myself that circumstances happen when you give attention to them through your thoughts. All doubts had disappeared, and now I decided to study and explore this concept in more depth.

5

The Revelation

After discovering this, what I would call a phenomenon, I started analyzing my life and that of others around me, scrutinizing my past and also the pasts of people I had known. I surmised without any further doubt that people had in their lives the reality of their thoughts. Whatever they expected life to deal them, it did. Ask and it is given. Looking back, I got the life I was asking for. Not intentionally. Had I known my years of sorrow were leading me to more, I would have made a greater effort to pull myself out of the darkness, if it was at all possible at the time. But now I know how to play the game; I am suddenly playing it very differently. I have learnt to think my way through life, accompanied by a feeling of ease. If you live in a world of pessimism and negativity, that is exactly what you get. Those who live in hope and faith receive it. Those who think wealth, prosperity, luck, they get that as well. If you think poor, sick, dwell on unwelcome incidents of the past, guess what? When I looked back on my own life and examined the pattern, I could not believe It! Things that I thought of did actually happen—simply by no other action than to think about it. What does all this mean? What you think, you receive. It's as simple as that. Well, that's not 100 per cent true, as a little more comes into play, which you will discover as you read; but you create your world through your thoughts.

You may be disagreeing. No one asks for a car accident, a deadly illness or for a house fire, etc. and you're right, they do not ask directly. Yet their thought patterns and emotions of anger, hate, stress, worry, negativity, frustration and more have brought about unwanted events indirectly that will be explained throughout the book. I ask you to keep an open mind and read on to understand it effectively so you can put it to good use and have it working for you, not against you. This book will help you to understand how unwanted events are occurring in your life and how to instead bring forth your desires.

If you have a spiritual basis, you may be thinking, this can't be true. Surely, there is stuff we have brought with us and come to experience. Certain people we meet along the way. Yes, I do believe that to be true. I do believe we have brought certain people and experiences with us but certainly not all of it; we have also come here to create and experience life. Those on a spiritual path tend to let the world take them to wherever without any conscious decisions, instead of making their own choices and having their own desires. With that, oftentimes you get caught up with everyone else's desires. You can still choose and create your own path without letting your spirituality fall by the wayside.

Once you start redirecting your thoughts to the way you want you and your life to be, you will start to take on miraculous changes in no time. Your thoughts will start having a profound effect on your relationships, health, the career you want, the home and car you desire, holidays; even your children will start putting up less resistance. You do not have to be smarter than anyone else to have a wonderful, prosperous life. That is probably the biggest problem for most. They equate success and happiness with smartness. There are many intelligent people who are far from happy and prosperous, and not all rich people were born with a silver spoon in their mouths. The problem is that people born into ordinary circumstances blame their upbringing for not having as much as others, but it is available to them. They simply have not worked out how to access it.

If it is your belief that this is all you can have in your life right now, that is the reason why you do not have more, even if you desire more. You do not believe you deserve more because you have not been encouraged to reach for more. You dwell on what is and fail to look beyond your negative thoughts that stand in the way of you getting what it is you truly desire. If you knew how toxic your negative thoughts are you will not be able to have another thought like it without being aware in an instant and redirecting your thinking immediately.

6

Influences and Mindsets

Our beliefs, desires, and our self-worth stem right back to the day we were born. All the influences in our life, both positive and negative, have an effect on how we view life. One observation I could not help but see the truth in is that many people tend to hang onto far more negative occurrences in their lives than the positive ones. We live in a negative world where so much more bad is pointed out than good, such as devastating world events right down to our own shortcomings. We have long forgotten the euphoria we felt during the Sydney 2000 Olympic Games but remember quite vividly the September 11 terrorist attack in 2001. We seem to thrive more on drama than we do pleasure. The recent Olympics in Rio was another perfect example. The media's coverage was so focused on the problems that more and more kept presenting themselves. Fires, thefts and other dramas constantly took away from the athletes achievements.

Take into account this story. When my son was about three years old, I used to tell him countless times to stay away from the iron while I was ironing as it was hot and if he touched it, he would burn himself. Naturally, I was only telling him this for his own comfort so he would not experience any pain. Out of curiosity he then put his whole hand on the iron. You could imagine the screaming and crying however, he never touched the iron again. His mind told him he had to experience the pain so he could appreciate life without it, and understand the pleasure of living pain free. It gave him more appreciation for his continual well-being. Being told it was painful wasn't enough, he had to experience it. Isn't that what we all do? If it takes pain in our lives to finally come to a place of joy, then that's the avenue we will take.

Probably the most impacting influence comes from having the actual of life's misfortunes pointed out to us. We have been conditioned by our previous generations to view life as a struggle and anything worth having we must grind ourselves into the ground for or it will not be as meaningful. We are taught that no one should have an easy path.

Our parents and preceding generations meant well, but it is sad to say they have probably had the greatest influence in our lives where our negative traits have been deeply ingrained within us. Yet it is not just our parents; it was most of our older generation, that thought by pointing out all our negative behavior, it would serve us well and also telling us all the bad things happening in the world, in the hope of protecting us. They were only trying to help you by making you aware of the evils out there so you could keep a lookout. But what they did not know was that by doing so, they were actually opening up the greater possibility of these incidences happening by activating your attention to them. Thus creating such fear, worry, and dread around you that you froze every time you had to make a decision or wanted to explore but were held back. You started to look at all the pitfalls when contemplating something new instead of the benefits. It's no wonder much of our society live in such fear and dread, and a large number of our population are on medication just to help them deal with life. Everyone is judging themselves after years of poor self-esteem caused by constantly being told they can do better or that they aren't trying hard enough, instead of being encouraged and being loved unconditionally.

Instead of being told how wonderful the world is and how wonderful they are, they were told of every conceivable thing that may go wrong in their lives. "Don't go out without a jacket and shoes, you will catch a cold." "Don't be silly on the swings, you will break a leg." "Be careful walking up the street, you will get mugged or run over.", "Don't talk to strangers, you will be stolen, raped or murdered." They only did what they knew, as this kind of conditioning had been instilled in them. You cannot teach something different if you have not learnt how or lack the desire to do so. That is because their upbringing was a great deal more detrimental to them than ours was to us. We at least have more awareness and tools to overcome this. Once we counteract this negative behavior by turning any negative into a positive, the difference will become your new reality. You just need to know where to start.

Think Before You Think has been designed to help you get off the merry-go-round of frustration and be able to have a simpler and wonderful life without having to constantly struggle for it. You will be able to let go of the worry of something going wrong as you will understand that only things that you think and worry about can happen to you. It will help you to understand why it is you are not getting what it is you desire, and how to turn this situation around. You deserve to have a fabulous life without the battles that generations before us endured. You are no less deserving than anyone else. You only think you are. We were brought up to think that life was supposed to be hard, that anything worth having had to be really worked hard for otherwise we would not appreciate it. If you did not put in the hard yards every time, you did not deserve to have it.

Your life is meant to be fantastic, so let's start erasing all the negative beliefs so you can start having the life you deserve. What has been instilled in you from previous generations is just a mindset; once you change that, the world is your oyster. Now, if you like struggle, and enjoy being under pressure, which is absolutely fine; don't change a thing. But if you are like me, wanting to enjoy all the pleasures of life, and make it all a bit simpler; keep reading. Throughout this book I want you to start realizing that a *belief is only a thought you keep thinking*. Once you get rid of those old beliefs, what you want will start to fall into place.

Let me ask you this question. Do you tend to have more negative day-to-day thoughts than positive ones? Do you tend to dwell on what someone did or said, how fat you are, how your life is unbearable, how you are going to pay the bills, or how you hate your job or how miserable you are, instead of something good? What do you think would happen if instead of having those negative thoughts, you gave your attention to the positive aspects of your life such as how nice people are to you, how well your kids are going, how healthy you are, how great it is going to be to go on that holiday and have the job, house or car you want? Once you have trained yourself to direct your thinking to thoughts of prosperity, happiness, appreciation, health, wealth and anything else you desire, you will eventually start getting them and your life is going to take off. In fact, the day you start doing this you will realize how much better it is to think pleasant thoughts rather than negative ones.

Life is a game; learn to play it to your advantage.

So how do you do that when you're in a dead end job you hate, the kids are playing up, you're up to your elbows in debt, and your partner has become more of an enemy instead of an ally? Start thinking of how you want life to be instead of how it currently is. Every time you keep wondering 'where is it?' you are counteracting your wishes.

Once you're aware that your thoughts are so much more powerful than your actions, you will start implementing more positive thoughts to get what you want instead of thinking you have to struggle your way through life. You will start seeing that with total trust and faith in your thinking; the right avenues will present themselves without you having to be forever looking for them. These miracles and more you will discover along the way and you will be so thankful for them.

7

Take a Look Back in Time

I want you to go back for a moment in time and observe certain events in your life. Go back as far as you can. When things did not turn out as you hoped, what were your thoughts or beliefs that led up to those events? Go back a few months, even a year or longer if you have to. I want you to take a moment and give this some real thought. Try and remember what your preceding thoughts were. Now do the same when things went well. What were your thoughts leading up to the incident? I bet when things went wrong you were not in a positive state of mind leading up to the events, and when you were, that is when situations turned out well for you. You were probably expecting things to go wrong. Now go back to people you know very well and do the same—your parents, siblings and good friends. Have you found a pattern?

I am sure you have. Have you wondered why people who are constantly thinking and talking of sickness are sick while those who focus on wellness are well? Those who focus on prosperity have it while those who think poor are? Granted, some people are born into a comfortable existence and others have great parental support or role models that have been a fantastic influence in their lives however, that is not always a prerequisite for a happy life. Some people from wealthy backgrounds may have all the material possessions they could want, yet that doesn't mean they have the relationships they would ultimately desire. Many materially successful people have lousy relationships, while many people with less have satisfying affiliations. Someone may have been taught how to attract money into their life, yet have not been shown how to attract great relationships. This is because we all have different needs as well as the fact that we don't know the principles behind why things are turning out the way they are.

Everyone is unique, and what may be important to one individual could be entirely worthless to another. So if money has been the target of your desire, you have probably learnt to do that well. If it is relationships, then that has probably been your main focus. The same with those who have great relationships without having material wealth; they have not been shown the know-how. Maybe those with sound relationships don't want material success or feel that having it is ungodly, or have a belief that you have to work too hard or sacrifice too much to have it. That is fine if you don't desire material success, but if you do the only thing stopping you from having it is you, your thoughts. If material success is a strong desire within you, don't feel guilty about it, no matter what you may have been told. We live in a physical and material world, and if we were not meant to have these, they would not have been created in the first place. Those that think being poor is somehow holy are incorrect. The intention of life is not about having to continually struggle, it's about abundance and prosperity in all areas. Material wealth is only detrimental if it controls you or your life and you believe it defines who you are.

8

Understanding How It Works

Nothing can happen in your life that you haven't wished for unless you have in some way allowed it in. Being unclear with your thoughts is one avenue for this to happen. The purpose of this book is to get you more focused on what it is you are thinking, to make your thoughts purposeful. Erase any worthless thinking and turn them into productive thoughts.

For you to start understanding this you have to realize you attract what you want through the vibration you are offering with your thoughts. All your thoughts are on a vibrational wavelength. You get what you think about. That is how the universe recognizes your desires. Your thoughts lead to feelings which emit a vibration that the universe recognizes. That means what is now in your life is a culmination of all your thoughts as well as the feelings you have had. You are where you are today not because of the thoughts you are thinking now but all your previous thoughts, some as far back as you can remember. Thoughts you have been clear on and at other times not so clear. That is why you have some, if not many things in your life you didn't particularly choose as you have not given enough attention to what you desire, so you have been dished up the thought patterns of people all around you.

I know you are going to find this hard to believe, and like me, it may take you months, possibly even years to start to realize this; however, whether you understand it or not, the law of attraction is always working. So wouldn't it be better to direct your thoughts to what it is you want instead of letting the universe dictate to you and bring you a mixed bag through your immediate surroundings? Have you noticed that when you feel out of control, everything seems to go wrong at the same time? The car breaks down, so does the washing machine, the hot-water system blows and unexpected bills pour in. This has not happened by chance.

Notice that people who have out-of-control lives also have out-of-control children, even their pets behave badly. They attract more out-of-control situations. Yet those who are happy and calm have children that are agreeable and pets that are perfect, everything falls into place for them. This is not by coincidence. You attract through your thoughts and to a lesser extent your actions. Have you also noticed when something has gone wrong you thought, "I knew that was going to happen," but that is not the case. You actually gave enough attention to it for it to become a reality.

9

Making the Changes

The good thing about bad things happening to you is that it gives you greater clarity to what it is that you do want. That is, negative events do serve you. If you didn't have the contrast of those events, you would not be able to greatly appreciate the good when it does come. The best thing that happened in your life is all those circumstances you didn't enjoy that made you reach for more. Be grateful for all those misgivings that have made you who you are today. Be resentful and you will only attract more of what you don't want. You would not be that person, or the person you're striving to become if those events did not take place. Cherish them and you are on the right path. That is why you quite often find people who have everything they could possibly want go off the rails for a while. They may have been born into wealth, fame and fortune. Life has been easy having everything given to them, so they have not appreciated it as much.

Once life takes a downward spiral, they start to grasp that their life was great and then do anything to get it back. They appreciate their life more as they have now experienced the contrast, and it is not so tolerable. A little bit of unhappiness goes a long way to helping us appreciate the good times. They may have also felt guilty having everything handed to them and through their guilt decided unconsciously to do it tough for a while. Once they understand that they have nothing to feel guilty about, they tend to reverse their perspective.

The situation can be much more challenging to deal with if they have undue pressure and expectations placed upon them to exceed or act a certain way. If this is the case, a person may go off the rails through rebellion or hate. Again, once they recognize the only person they are truly hurting is themselves, oftentimes they manage to turn their life around. That is why so many people need to hit rock bottom before they start working their way back up again. They know there is nothing in that black hole and the only way is up, but they need to surrender and give up the fight before they are able to claw their way back.

The first change you need to make is the vibrational pattern you have been offering probably since you were a child. Whether you are aware of it or not, you have many influences and beliefs that have been ingrained in you all your life. Many of them are not even yours however, because at the time you didn't know better, or were not allowed your own opinion, they are there. You may not have those old influences around you as much anymore, but the imprint remains and; more often than not, you are now starting to pass those beliefs onto your own children and others around you. That is because you have been living many years with these belief patterns that they have been ingrained within you. The only way to change it is to at first recognize it and make the effort to do so.

I am sure you are aware of the sayings, *birds of a feather flock together, like attracts like* and *the law of attraction*. These words are so much more profound than you could possibly be aware of. Your world is surrounded by people and places that are like-minded to you. You are constantly attracting circumstances, people and events through your thoughts; some you do not want in your existence but while you keep focusing on them, they are still there.

So why are you not getting what it is you want? There are many reasons for this. Just the act alone of wanting it and not believing is enough to not allow it in. Factor in feelings of guilt, self-worth, feeling undeserving, fear, inadequacy, rejection, impatience, and focusing on the lack of your desires, these will all push what you want away instead of towards you. This is easy to overcome when you start to understand why you have these beliefs and alter your thoughts to ones that will allow them to flow.

Let's start with guilt. Many people feel guilty about desiring more as they have been conditioned with the notion you should be grateful with what you have and not want for more. Be thankful that you have a job, a roof over your head and the children are healthy. That you are being selfish asking for more. And why should you have more? Everyone else is struggling, why should your life be easy? Many of you think that your lives should be difficult because your parents' lives were and so is that of most people around you. If yours is easy, people will perceive you as lazy, hence the guilt. So you should cram so much into your day that by the end of it you will feel so exhausted, just like the rest of them. That way you will feel confident that you have accomplished some great achievement, and then you won't feel so bad. But see, like attracts like. That is why most of your friends and family are in the same boat as you are. You can break the mold if you want to, but you need to choose to. If it makes you happy to exhaust yourself every day, keep doing it. If not, stop and let go of the guilt.

There is nothing wrong with feeling great satisfaction in sacrificing to have something that you have worked really hard for. There is a great sense of achievement when you have toiled away to reach a goal. However, if there are times you wish for things to be a little easier instead of having to struggle and sacrifice every time you want something, you have to learn how to jump off the merry-go-round. So first decide, do you want to be exhausted and stressed all the time or would you rather be happy? And how do you jump off this merry-go-round you have been on for so long? You have to break your pattern of thought; start thinking of how you would like your life to be instead of how it is. More information is given in the proceeding chapters; but once your thoughts change, the events will too.

Many of you think that you are undeserving, not smart enough, or don't work hard enough to have the good life. While that is your belief it is exactly what it is that you get. I can tell you though there are many people out there who would have less intelligence than you that are wealthy, prosperous, and living like a king. Why? They believe they deserve it so they get it. Opportunities come their way because they are open to them. They can see an opportunity, and when they do, they take it; they are not overridden with fear or doubt. They don't think about what could go wrong; they focus on what will go right. They don't believe they have to work seventy hours a week to have success, but if you do, then you must, for you only get what it is you believe. Sure, work long hours at your job if you are passionate about it and it is your love, but if not change it. How, you ask? First recognize that the belief came from somewhere else; more than likely your parents.

Are you focusing on the solution or the problem?

You may have been told to have anything good you have to work really hard, save and sacrifice, and if you're lucky, eventually it will come. Plenty of people have made millions from one simple idea they had and are living the high life off the royalties. You may think you are not smart enough to come up with an idea that could make you a fortune. If you think like that, you won't. Maybe you don't want to have a million dollar idea. That is fine too. Decide what it is you want and it will come to you. Read the *"Money and Careers"* chapter for a better understanding of this.

By looking at the negative reason why you want something, such as having more money will mean you will not be poor anymore, you are not allowing a positive energy to bring it to you. Whenever you are in a state of needing something your desire will not eventuate. Your neediness holds your desires away from you. It is exactly the same principle as when someone feels needy around people. Don't you notice how needy people repel other people away from them? It's the same when you want something that bad you feel you must have it or your life will be in tatters. The frequency you are offering is not allowing your desire in no matter how much you are striving to achieve it. You are pushing your desires away from you. You have to come to a place of least resistance to allow desires to flow. Another way to put this is, when someone has been trying to achieve a certain goal or desire for so long but to no avail. Once they 'give up' they have released the pressure surrounding the situation, and once this happens often their object of desire follows. But there is no such thing as giving up as the desire is still there; they have just let go of the pressure surrounding it.

To bring something that you want into your life, you must focus on the great reasons for having it. Thoughts such as more money will allow you to choose which job you prefer to do, give you more time with your family, be able to take the children on exciting outings, have more holidays or have a bigger house so the kids all have their own rooms. These are all positive reasons for wanting more money, and constant thoughts like that will eventually line it up your desires for you and it then must be bought into your life. But thoughts of "I don't deserve it," "Good things don't come to me," "I wouldn't know what to do with all that money," "I am sick of living like this,", or "How much longer do I have to wait?", all these thoughts will hold it away from you. You also counteract the desire or desires by not believing you will get it or not deserving of receiving them.

The biggest detriment to any aspiration is the attention of it not being in your life yet and focusing on the lack of it. Believing that it will never come and that you are just kidding yourself only kills your dream. When you are constantly pointing out why it is not in your life, the reason it is not eventuating is that you are holding it outside of you. The energy you are offering will not allow it in. Understand that once you have put a desire forward, you must be in a place of receiving it, and the universe has to do its work as well to position it into your life.

The greatest benefit to you is to keep thinking about the desire that you have. Hold it there in the back of your mind. The other key is to make sure you feel good about these thoughts. Keep thinking about it in a positive manner until it eventually turns up in your life. But remember, every time you think of its absence or are feeling anxious about when it will present itself you are counteracting the thought. Let's say you have to think of something two hundred times before it comes into your life, but you have negative thoughts around it half of the time. That means you have to have one hundred more productive thoughts before it comes. That is why it can take so long or does not come at all as you keep on counteracting it. Once you have put your wish out there, know it will come to you, but you must go about your life in a state of expecting it and enjoying the moment you have now and not constantly being disappointed it hasn't yet materialized.

Many are also looking for the pitfalls. They are so concerned that once they get their wish, it could be taken away from them just as quickly, so they think maybe they should not want it in the first place.

Unless they change this belief, this is exactly what will happen, as you get what you think about. If you think it will fall apart, it will.

Do not think that anything is too big for you to have. If you have a strong desire for it and it makes you feel good, it will be yours if you are receptive to it, whether it is a thousand dollars or a million, your dream job or a partner—anything at all. You need to remember that anything and everything that has materialized in this world was a thought before it appeared—every desire, concept and innovation. The only limitation is you. You may think that to have what you want you have to wait a long time, work very hard, go without, or make great sacrifices. This is certainly going to be the case if you think like that. Change your belief to a new one such as things come easily to you, you deserve to have everything that you desire.

A good analogy around this subject would be a new job you have started. On your first day you would have felt totally out of place, as if you didn't know what was going on and you felt you were out of your depth. But day by day, week by week, you started to ease into it until a month or a few down the track it was as if you had been there for years. You have settled right in and feel comfortable in your new role. You now know your job without having to give too much thought to it. It is the same when you are learning to drive a car. You have to think of every move you make, change the gears, put your foot on the pedal, indicate, and brake. Years later, you do not give any of that a second thought. You have conditioned your mind to driving.

The same goes for any a desire you deem to be too big right now. Just keep giving it more thought until it feels really comfortable to you and it could easily slip right into your life. This will start to become your new reality. Chances are that is when it will manifest, as you have lined yourself up with your desire.

I am not saying that thinking alone will get you everything you desire as action does need to be applied (but certainly not always), you do need to be moving in the direction of your goal with the right attitude. Having said that, mere thinking brings about the results in your life—both positive and negative. The benefit of thought and its influence on your life works like this…If your thoughts are of a positive nature, opportunities will be bought into your life from which you can take action that will have resonated with your thinking. You will find opportunities appearing: however, it does work in reverse. Should your thoughts be negative, by the principles of the universe, you will find situations appearing in your life that are not to your liking.

Training Your Mind

You are a culmination of all your previous thoughts. You are where you are today from years of thoughts and the vibration you have been offering to the universe. You may not be where you want to be, that is because you have not been clear enough with your thoughts to be exactly where you would like. Most of your thoughts do not manifest instantly. If that was the case, we would spend so much of our time cleaning up the things we didn't want and the mistakes that come with careless thinking. That is why there is a buffer period between what it is you want and your desires coming to fruition. This buffer gives you the necessary timeframe required to let go of any negative thought before your thinking manifests, and give more clarity to what it is that you want.

You may desire a new car, but if it came in an instant, you would not have had ample time to consider the color, shape, size, model, engine size, and other features. The car that turns up today would most certainly be inappropriate for your lifestyle; you have not chosen with much thought to it. Once you decide you would like a new car, go about thinking of all the features you would like that car to have. That way you will know when the right car for you comes along. So it is really important to start directing your thoughts in the direction you want to go. It is the same with a partner. If you were to think today "I want a new partner", you would get the first person who is walking past. That is not what you want! You want to be able to choose a person with the right traits for you such as personality, looks, character, beliefs and whatever else you are looking for in a mate. If you focus on all the aspects you desire, the right mate will eventually show. You just have to be clearer about what it is you desire in anything. Remember, you have had years of thought, vibrations, and beliefs, so you need to change them if you want to improve your life.

A belief is just a thought you keep thinking.

Be aware that any strong thoughts that you have had, negative or positive, will most likely still materialize into your life due to the years of attention you have been giving them. If they are things that you want, keep thinking of them. If they are things that you don't want, do not give them your attention any more. A few months after a frustrating time in my life I received a large parking fine by mistakenly parking in a disabled zone, had a minor car accident as well as endless bills pouring in. I started to think that my new beliefs must be untrue because if my thoughts were becoming more focused, how could this be happening? However, after I pulled myself out of my frustration and took a step back, I came to see that these were all my old thoughts surfacing; I was facing the reality of my past thoughts. I just had to grin and bear that period of my life and ride through it until my new thoughts started appearing into my reality. You will find that many people who feel under stress in their jobs get sick the moment they take holidays and relax. It is the same principles at work; so do be patient and don't give up before you have a chance to see the benefits. The most important part of this stage was not to get frustrated with the reality and accept it. If you have a negative response you will create more of it.

The first aspect of creating a new way of thinking is to stop thinking about what it is you do not want. The more attention you give to your unwanted experiences, the higher the likelihood they will appear in your life. It does not serve you to focus on what it is you don't want; stop thinking about any experiences that have hurt you, or anything that has not worked out for you. By dwelling on them, you are keeping the problem in your energy field and bringing more of the same to you. Remember, the law of attraction will keep bringing more of it to you as it acts like a snowball effect. Negative thought brings more negative thought upon more. *Stop.* The only way for you to move forward is to put the event in the past and focus on the life that you want. The event does not have to be a big one for it to still be hindering you. It may be a comment made to you when you were young, an incident of late, a friend that deceived you or a health issue you keep talking about to anyone who will listen. It may be of a much greater capacity, but until you can put any negative incident in the past it will always hinder your future.

The best way to stop thinking about a negative incident is to think of something else. This is because you cannot tell yourself to stop thinking about something, as while you're not trying to think about it you are still giving it your attention. When something bad has happened, the best way to deal with this is to reverse it into how you would like the situation to be. Examples of this are: if you are working in a job you don't like, you want to be working in a job that gives you satisfaction. If you are feeling unsafe or have been violated, safety is what you desire. If you are sick, you would like to be well. If you are poor, you would like to be better off. There is always an opposite of any problem, and that is the solution; so focus on the positive opposite of the situation. If you dwell on an experience you don't want to have in your life, you are giving it more substance and bringing more of it in.

You and only you are the creator of your own experience. Once you accept this, take accountability for your life and stop blaming others. Each time you have a thought of revenge, what someone did or said to you, or how you were harmed, you are wasting precious thinking time that could be used so much more productively. If you are thinking past thoughts that do not involve love or appreciation, stop dwelling on them. There is nothing in your past that has happened that can be changed, no matter how awful. It does not assist you to hold onto it so do yourself a favor and let it go; you are only damaging yourself and your future, not to mention those around you, such as your children and partner. Start using your thoughts wisely; think about how you want things to be and not how they were. In time, it will change. It is all practice. If you don't, the hurt will keep eating at you until you have an insidious disease such as cancer. Constantly thinking about what you don't want will only bring you more of it. If you want to erase it, you have to change your thoughts.

Remember, you have been thinking your thoughts for many, many years. You are today living proof of all your previous thoughts, some of which have not even manifested yet. What are you thinking now, is it of benefit to you? If not, change it, as it will eventually show up in the future. That means there are past thoughts you have had up to a year ago (possibly longer) that have not yet surfaced in your reality. It may turn up today, tomorrow, next week, or next month. That is why there is a buffer of time between what you think today and how long it takes to show up, so you can have time to clean up your thoughts and become more precise in your desires. Something that you keep thinking over and over again will show up eventually.

Recognize that when these do materialize, this is old stuff you were thinking. If these events do occur, and your reaction to them is negative, it will only add to more detriment down the track, and you don't want that. Deal with it as best you can. Also, don't wait for them to happen, as you will only be giving them more power. Keep having your positive thoughts, and in a matter of time, if you have really made an effort to change the way you think, you will start to see how your life has taken on a new reality.

Stay away from people who will not be supportive of you. The last thing you need while you are at the beginning stage of redirecting your thoughts is to have pessimists around you that could hinder your progress. Eventually, once your vibration becomes strong enough, those people will play a much lesser role in your life as like attracts like, and your positive outlook will start to become boring to them. They will start gravitating to other like-minded people. You will find that soon enough; you will attract more like-minded people into your life. But in the meantime, if they can't be supportive of your new-found outlook, keep it to yourself. You can still be upbeat and positive; just don't divulge anything to them that will attract a negative response, discouraging you from your new outlook.

People don't like others that are moving in a different direction to them as it makes them feel like they are being left behind. If they don't choose to catch up, then that is their choice. When they want to talk about topics with negative overtones, change the subject or don't offer an opinion. By joining them, you are undoing your good work, for it is most important to not invite those unwanted experiences into your existence, and merely being around them can be enough if you happen to start contemplating on any level what it is they are discussing. A perfect example is the health industry. Anyone who works in the health industry or gets caught up in the emotion of their work is likely to contract some kind of illness.

Your job is not to change the world or other people around you; that is their responsibility. Let them create their own life. They may see the change in you and your life and will either want to embrace it or feel threatened by it. That is their choice. Be a role model for those around you, especially your children. That is the best thing you can do for anyone. Those who do not wish to will not want to spend as much time in your company, and I can assure you, you will not miss them.

Money

re you one of the many who wish you had more money in your life? Then you are not alone. Talk to just about anyone and their greatest desire is almost always to have more money. Money gives people freedom and more choices to choose from.

I mentioned that at times I can be materialistic, and in all honesty that has not changed. I like knowing that I can afford to pay my mortgage instead of struggling to try and find the repayments each month. I enjoy knowing that I can go out and have lobster if I choose to or lunch with a friend instead of having to live on sausages and tinned food. I enjoy all my luxuries, such as massage or a pedicure and knowing I can help someone in need, instead of worrying if I will have enough until the next pay check.

After going through a period in my life when maybe I was a little too materialistic, I thought I should not place so much emphasis on money, however I soon decided that wasn't the answer either. Having had a partner for period of time that lived from week to week, I soon became aware that going without doesn't make you happy. There is nothing wrong with wanting to be abundant materially. We live in a material world. Happiness has a different meaning for everyone, and I can attest I would rather be well off and unhappy than poor and unhappy.

Unless you have a healthy relationship with money, it will be extremely hard to allow more of it into your existence. Money needs to be treated like any relationship, with respect. Treat it too frivolously or hold onto it to tightly, and money will soon escape from your grasp. If you think that money causes more problems than it is worth or that anyone who has a vast amount of money must have earned it in some deceitful way, you are not allowing more of it to come to you. If you have any of these thoughts in regard to money, ask yourself why? It is more than likely that your conditioning around money has come from those around you such as your parents and other adult influences. You probably would have heard those influences talk often about how money does not grow on trees or that people with wealth can't be trusted.

To allow more money into your life you need to alter that kind of thinking and look at the benefits having more money would bring into your life instead of the negatives that the lack of it brings. Remember, it's not the rich people that are robbing banks, stealing cars or breaking into homes to pay for their lifestyle. People with wealth have just worked out the secret of how to have money constantly coming their way. They may be earning much more than you but they are not working that much harder, nor are they that much smarter, we all only have 24 hours in a day.

Think of the benefit more money would bring not only to your life but also those around you. It's hard to help someone in need of money when you don't have any to give, so start believing you deserve to have money. The universe has not left you behind and picked someone more deserving over you; you have. You deserve to have a life free of struggle just as much as anyone, but if you think you have to work really hard to have money, then that is exactly how it will be. If you think that you need to be really smart to be rich and you have to come up with some whiz bang idea for it to come to you, then that will be your truth. Once you change this mindset, money or anything else for that matter will come easily. There are plenty of school dropouts who have made millions of dollars, just as there are many intelligent people who have gone to university for eight years that have hardly anything. I am sure you know somebody whose life seems magical and everything always falls into place without much effort. It has nothing to do with being lucky, they simply send out the right energy to get it.

Start seeing yourself leading the life in which you desire. Once you keep saying and picturing it time and time again, your resistance will break down and you will feel good about it, getting ready to allow it in. Start putting pictures in your mind of the kind of home you wish to live in, imagine the kind of job you would like and the lifestyle you desire. At first, it will feel a little awkward and out of place, but after a while it will feel so natural, and when it does come, it will fit perfectly. It's your job once you have done these things to let go and let these opportunities make their way to you.

Tell yourself you attract money to you.
Money comes easily to you.

If you concern yourself with too many of the details of how it might present itself, you will start putting up resistance and stall the process. You simply need to be open to how it will unfold. It may be from a large pay rise, a change in employment, or a redundancy with a huge payout. It may be a lottery win, investment opportunity or an inheritance. You may find an idea you come up with; it doesn't matter how. Don't focus on how or when it will come unless there is something that you really want to do; otherwise you will stifle the avenues of how it is likely to present itself. You will know the right avenue when it appears as it will feel right. The more attention you give to it and the more passion that you put around it without the resistance, the faster it will come. But don't counteract your dreams by wondering why it hasn't happened yet, that will only stall the process. Go about your life and focus on the positive aspects you are living.

If you want a million dollars and you earn $50,000 a year, it would take you more than twenty years to save. However, if you focus on the reality of that fact, you will only get your truth. If instead you only focus on the goal and feel excited about the outcome, it will take you a lot less time and with hardly any effort. Just believe you deserve it. You may see an advertisement for a kind of job you feel compelled to go for, or maybe some new direction with a job opportunity or it may be some other avenue. If it is meant to be, it will be easy; if not, you will be met with all types of barriers to say that is not the right way. But don't think you have to keep constantly searching for it; it will find you. Your constant action of trying to find it will only push the opportunity further away due to your desperation to change your present circumstances.

Most people feel guilty if they were to come into a large amount of money, as they feel would be depriving another, but there is plenty of money being exchanged around the world every day, there is never going to be a shortage. There is enough of everything in the world. There is abundance everywhere, in everything, including our resources. You are only told that there is a shortage so you continue to live in fear and people in power will have control over you. Those who need more money do have access to it. They simply need to change their mindset around money to allow more to flow into their lives.

There was a time when I would think of very rich people as being greedy, being surrounded by so much opulence when there are so many less fortunate who could use it. Then I started to think differently. I turned my thinking around to when they spend their fortunes on their extravagances, I thought of the jobs and opportunities they were creating for others through the spending of their vast wealth. I soon came to a peaceful place over this issue.

You may feel guilty when you spend money and buy something that you think maybe you shouldn't. Each time you make a purchase you are helping to support someone else, therefore stimulating the economy. Every service you use, each product you buy, whether it is in your country or not goes to help pay staff, people they lease from, the utility companies that employ people, the delivery drivers, the cleaners and so on. And the money you spend, they spend and help someone else and then the next person spends and helps someone else who all have families.

Take a note or a coin out of your wallet or purse and have a look at the date. Think about how much time it spends in your possession and now imagine the age of it and how many hands and tills it has gone through in its life. Money is like water, it keeps on running. Think of it as a baton in a relay that never ends, quite an amazing thought. We are also encouraged to buy locally to help our own, however keep in mind those overseas distributors who have families as well and many of them do not have the same opportunities we have here. So the next time you have a manicure, pedicure, eat out or treat yourself, buy something that you may never use, give some thought to who you are helping. This way you will feel better when you hand over your cash, and when it feels better, you are making way for more of it to come back to you.

I want to tell you some stories in regards to a few investments I tried to make. My focus has always been on how to make money, not whether or not an investment may be risky. I was looking to buy an old house in a country town that was zoned for development. To my surprise I could not get the loan; I tried several different avenues, even to purchase jointly with my son, but to no avail. I found out not long after that the property prices in that particular area took a tumble after my applications were declined. Another time, I wanted to buy some shares on the internet. Each time I went to proceed with the transaction the phone would ring or I would be interrupted. Not long after the share market crashed. Yet another time, I was trying to sell an investment property interstate so I could stop renting and purchase my own home. I was dismayed that the sale took over six months. However, over that period of six months I made an extra $50,000 on the property I was selling, and the area I wanted to live in fell dramatically in price when I was buying. My home loan that would have been for so much more was now only a fraction of that.

Now, if I at any time had any concern of losing money, all the transactions that I had trouble with would have gone through easily. Other property I had owned with others had not performed nearly as well as the ones that I owned by myself, as their attention to the possibility of losing money stood directly in the way. When you have faith, everything works in your favor. There is so much behind-the-scene stuff you cannot see at the time but trust it will work out for you.

I would like to say that the reason for my success was because of some skilful know-how on my part, but if the truth be known my success came because I intended on making money and the right opportunities were brought to me.

Health

No one ever says that they want to be sick or unwell. They don't say, "Today I think I will have cancer or AIDS." Yet the way we live and think about life brings these kinds of illnesses and diseases on.

Any negative emotion you feel will more than likely have a negative impact on your health, if you dwell on it long enough. Most people think that health problems, whether it be sickness or an injury happen by chance, but they could not be further from the truth. Why do you hear of people who have always been so healthy suddenly dying of a heart attack or in a car accident? How does someone who has smoked and drunk all their life live a healthy life until 100? It is no mistake. I believe that ill health or injury is brought about by matters of the mind.

Think of anyone you know who has ill health or a serious injury, and it is highly likely they are either holding onto a past hurt, are full of anger, rage, resentment, lack self-worth or are concerned about being unwell. This also applies to anyone who is a constant worrier. Things that we do not want happen to us when we are angry, resentful, vulnerable, worried, and the like. When we are feeling any of these emotions, it is highly likely we are going to attract ill health over time if we continue the current thought patterns. Illness and injury is the body's way of letting you know something is your life is not right, so pay attention and listen.

Some illnesses may be hereditary, but even in this situation I believe the problem would usually lay dormant and will not raise its ugly head until some sort of stress has been placed on the body to give it reason to come to light. Constant worry or concern of getting some kind of illness will also manifest it into existence.

If there is a history of disease or illness, the reason why it tends to be passed on through the generations is the constant fear of getting it. The more you worry and talk about it, keep having constant check-ups, the more chance you have of contracting the illness as your thought processes are holding onto it. Then you say, 'Oh, it's hereditary'. At times, heredity problems do not arise or may skip a generation, and I put this down to being in tune with your mind and life. An illness may lay dormant all this time and surface when you are out of alignment with your thoughts.

The same goes for an injury. If you think you are going to hurt yourself, you more than likely will. If you have negative thoughts while you are doing something, chances are an injury could occur. When I have hurt myself, stubbed a toe, or stabbed myself with something, I have immediately asked myself what it was that was in my thoughts at the time, and it has always been something negative. These kinds of accidents almost always happen when you are having a negative thought.

Anyone who breaks a leg or an arm, or has some sort of injury that lays them up has more than likely been telling themselves on some level that they need a rest or a change in direction. Maybe they have not been enjoying what they it is they have been doing or are feeling exhausted and fed up, then bingo; an injury occurs to prevent them from what it is they have wanted to avoid. Not long ago I kicked my foot and broke a few toes. I thought of the inconvenience it will put on my work load however, when I gave more thought to it, I realized I was not enjoying what I was doing and had been given a reason to not be able to do it.

An injury may have occurred because you never feel safe and believe you are prone to injury and accidents. Your wish is the universe's command. Where a child is concerned, you may have been constantly telling a child not to do a particular activity, that they will get hurt or break a bone. You have put the thought into their head. If they do it enough it could then occur, and it does if they persist on doing that task. Sick children normally have problems adjusting to life, they may not enjoy school, feel pressured, or have poor self-esteem or feel high levels of anxiety for some reason. My sister always felt she was the least loved, and she was the one that suffered with asthma and pneumonia.

As a general rule, cancer comes about by having something eating at you by way of anger, resentment, repressed feelings, etc. Smaller nuisances such as boils, ingrown toenails, reappearing sores and the like is usually an indication of small issue bugging you, festering within you. Rashes, allergies, etc. are normally a sign you are doing something that you do not want, or that is not in alignment with your desires. You may be exhausted or frustrated with a situation. If you want to stay safe and healthy, get in alignment with yourself. Car accidents can be a way of getting you to change an area of your life. Minor accidents mean minor change, and major ones could be major issues. All the car accidents I have had in my life came at a time when I was already in a crisis! Heart attacks and strokes are a huge build-up of stress, anger, or resentment. These are all general statements but when you come across some kind of health issue, give thought as to whether you need to change your thoughts or an aspect of your life.

Of course, if you think that you will be sick, you will eventually make yourself sick. If you think every winter you will get the flu, chances are not a winter will go by when you don't catch it. My mother was constantly being told if she didn't take better care of herself, she would get diabetes and have her leg amputated, which is eventually what happened. People often ask me if she had her leg amputated due to having diabetes, however, my belief is that the resentment, anger and regret she held onto for years was the primary cause, and the other was secondary to that, not to mention people putting the idea in her head. While mum was in rehab all the nurses were pleading with her to have the flu vaccination. Mum vehemently refused to have it. She knew she didn't need it because she was confident she would never get the flu, and she never did.

I have a good friend who is a walking encyclopedia on health and illness. If you had the symptom, she would be able to give you a correct diagnosis before you even went to the doctor. The problem was that even though she was obsessed with her own exercise and eating regime, she was one of the most unwell people I knew. More often than not, she is sick as opposed to being well. In her fascination with medicine and diagnosing others, she was not aware she was bringing about her own illnesses by giving her constant attention to diseases and the like.

A dear relative of mine who works in the field of health has so much compassion and concern for her clients. I have no doubt that is why she quite often ill herself. Her love and care for them I believe enter into her field of energy, and although she is the fittest of all her friends and the one who takes the best care of herself, she has a number of health problems that the rest of her 'less healthy' friends don't have.

*One thought attracts another and then
another. What thoughts are you attracting?*

If you are ill or have an injury and don't think you will recover, you probably won't. As hard as it is with the being sick and in pain, if you keep focusing on it, it will take longer to heal, if ever. If you are in a position of ill health, it can be difficult to focus on wellness through the pain and lethargy. Just try and distract yourself as best you can. Do anything that you can to take your attention off the pain, whether it is having people and animals around you, meditating, reading, sleeping, and more importantly seeing yourself as being well. Anything at all that is going to make you feel good. Spend some time as you can every day visualizing what it would be like to have your health back, that you can feel yourself healing from the inside out. See yourself as being carefree and well again. Disregard any negative thoughts that you may have when they pop into your mind and think about things that only make you cheerful. I have heard many stories of people becoming well by being surrounded by laughter and humor—anything that will put you in a positive frame of mind will be of benefit to you.

I have no doubt that eventually people will catch on to how much impact their thinking has on their health and over time will be more aware to think in a constructive manner. When this happens the stress on our health system will start to ease. A healthy mind leads to a healthy body; however, it does not work the other way around. A healthy body will eventually become diseased if the mind is not.

Prevention in the first place is definitely better than finding a cure.

Depression

P   *lease note: This is general information only and may be helpful for those with the onset of depression. If necessary, it is recommended to seek medical attention and /or contact Lifeline or the equivalent in your area.*

It can be very, very hard to see the bright side of anything when you feel angry, depressed and confused. I have been in that state and I'm sure just about everyone has been at some time in their life, when you cannot seem to find a way out of the black hole and everything looks doomed. Yet your constant attention to these thoughts and feelings that you have are only going to attract more of the same, so you have to find a way to feel better. It is a must for your situation to improve, even if you have to fantasize about how you would like your life to be in an ideal world. That is what all this is about anyway—thinking your way to a better life. No matter what your situation is, if you focus on how you want things to be, your circumstances can only improve. Eventually, the right people will cross your path as long as you believe they will come. Do not focus on how the situation will turn or when, just trust that it does. If you hold onto a time frame you are in fact setting the time back longer due to placing extra pressure on the situation and yourself. You will find people and circumstances will be sent to you when you just let go and allow it to happen. Of course, there are going to be times when you fall off the wagon and sink back. Do not despair and dwell there, telling yourself that it is no good. Just have your moment and then lift yourself up. Also do not try to get from being depressed to a state of euphoria, the emotions are way too far apart and in no time you will feel even worse. Just take each day as it comes, even though I know you want to try and pull yourself out of it as quickly as you can. Unfortunately it is a gradual process due to the huge difference in the emotions you have been feeling.

Once you start to have some happy thoughts, more will follow and then some more and more again. You see, it is the law of attraction. The circumstances surrounding you now are there because you keep thinking about them and dwelling on them. Do whatever you have to do to change your thoughts. Pat a pet, do a good deed, watch a funny movie, read an uplifting book, listen to happy music, start a hobby, sleep if you have to. Helping someone else almost always makes you feel good about yourself as you will be purposeful. Just distract yourself. Try and do something useful. Know it will eventually change once you start changing your thoughts and feelings around the situation. If you keep telling yourself you suffer from depression, anxiety, etc, you always will. Everyone is the creator of their own lives, including you, so make an effort to change it, if that is your want.

Often depression is caused from having expectations unmet. You want something in your life to be a certain way and it isn't, and you have no idea to get where it is you want to go or to achieve what it is you want. You more than likely have inbuilt anger which has been internalized to cause depression. The best thing you can do is to give up on the situation causing you this grief. Giving up and surrendering to the problem will cause a release in your body. It may not feel good, as if life has control over you however, after a few weeks of this you will feel like a huge weight has been lifted.

When you are miserable, you attract more misery into your life; everything you witness around you will be covered in a grey cloud. You are attracting more people who are in a similar state to you. It may feel good to be surrounded by like-minded people, satisfied that you are not going through this alone, but you will never lift yourself out if you decide to keep focusing there. You think to yourself that your life is surrounded by misery, and it must mean that you are meant to live a miserable life, but that is not the case; your misery is attracting more. As hard as it is when you are feeling low, you have to try with all your might to find something that makes you feel better. In time you will start attracting more joyous circumstances to you, and you will be on your way to being a more positive and optimistic person with a new and improved life.

While you are in this low state, you will find you will keep attracting similar, depressing situations over and over again, almost like you are jinxed or cursed. It is imperative that each time you have a negative event take place in your life that you do not say to yourself, "Here we go again!" or have any negative kind of reaction to the problem. If you do the same issue will keep on reoccurring. You must not have any negative reaction at all and in time, these events that keep on bringing you down will eventually disappear. However, I cannot stress enough just how important this part of the process is.

14

Weight Control and Addictions

have put the issue of weight control and addictions together as I believe that many of the same mindsets cause the same issues and similar principles and techniques can help to overcome them. Both are trying to control a substance; the only difference is that food is something we can't live without.

Firstly, I would like to explain addictions in a simple analogy in regard to the law of attraction. Let's take alcohol for instance. The very first time you ever have one or two drinks, you are going to feel the effects, possibly be drunk, have a hangover, or both. However, after a while if you continue to drink, your body adjusts to the dosage and eventually you are able to drink more and more until you have the same after-effect. A little bit like the law of attraction. The more you pay attention to it, the more you get used to it; it becomes a habit. Remember, if you think happy thoughts, you will have more, they are drawn to you. If you keep drinking or taking any other substance, the more you take, the more you will get used to it, the more you will attract situations that are similar. If this is the case you will probably recognize you have attracted more alcoholic friends or you are mixing with people who like to drink or do drugs.

The first step to making a change is to put the intention forward. Tell yourself over and over you want to be sober, drug free, have a healthier body or less body weight (whatever it is you choose), and you, in time, will start to attract some situations that will make the process easier for you. You may run into someone who has had a similar problem, or you come across someone who may be your support buddy. You could stumble across a new clinic or programme that would help. Remember, your attention to wanting the improved situation will bring the solution into your life and necessary opportunities to help you through it. However, your concern of otherwise will keep the potential support at bay. In the meantime, you need to picture yourself being how it is you want to be, even if you are still 'using' at the time.

To help condition your mindset it is a good idea to spend some time every day in a quiet, uninterrupted space. Try and do as often as time permits. Sit or lie down and put some quiet music on if you wish. Relax and breathe, in and out slowly. If you have heard a meditation CD and know the technique of starting to relax your head, neck, shoulders, right down to your toes, use that. You don't need a CD, you can say it to yourself in your mind. The whole idea is for you to become more relaxed and let go of any thoughts. Do this for a few minutes, then imagine you are walking down a staircase, slowly counting backward from ten each time you step on one. Then imagine yourself in a pleasant setting of your choice. Have a good look around at the scenery. Picture the scene and the new you—the weight that you wish to be or having control of your addictions. See yourself sober, talking to people, look around you at the setting. See who is with you. Make up a conversation and see yourself talking to people. Soak in the happiness you are feeling having everything under control. You are in more control of your life. Stay in that scene for as long as you want, and when you are ready, slowly bring yourself around. Set time aside to do this every day so it becomes a habit and the images are reinforced in your mind.

Now start the programme when you feel ready. If you are not ready, that's fine; try cutting down or only 'use' every alternate day. The thought of giving up a habit can be most daunting. Simply cutting back is a great way to start. Anything is an achievement. Just do what make you feel happy and what you think is best for you. If you slip, do not beat yourself up. It's the beating yourself up that is bringing all the good work undone. You think "What's the use, I will never kick this." and poof, 'your wish is thy command'. Just get back on board the next day. Look at a slip this way. Let's say you are used to drinking twelve units of alcohol a day, every day. You have done exceptionally well and gone without for five days, but on day six you have reverted back to twelve. That means you went without alcohol for five days, which is sixty units less than normal. That is great, a fantastic effort. Don't berate yourself;

be proud. You may be able to get it in the first go or it may take you many; just keep trying.

If you feel that by telling people you will put extra pressure on yourself, then don't. You may think their attitude is 'Yeah, yeah, how many times have I heard that before?' Those kinds of remarks will only make you doubt yourself. However, if you feel you need support and can trust the person to be in your corner, go ahead. Do what feels good to you. You will start to notice, if you really want to overcome some problem; the right people and support programs will cross your path.

One aspect I myself have always found difficult to control is my weight. Ever since I was young I remember always thinking that whenever I put food in my mouth it would make me fat. Being reminded of that constantly by my elders in no way helped and hence my issue around the subject now. All my life I have had the belief that I have to exercise often and always be hungry if I wanted to maintain my ideal body weight. However, the sacrifice to me always seemed too great. One morning, I woke up really wanting some solution to this ongoing problem, so I quietly asked for a way to reach a weight I was happy with without having to feel I was punishing myself. That week I came across a few people who introduced me to methods I had not tried before, and have been successful. In the past, I would have dismissed these methods had I not been aware of what it was I was asking for, and I would have missed the signs. But knowing what I now know, I knew these people came to me because I asked. I have tried various weight loss fads in the past, many that have worked for others yet not for me. The reason for this, I have surmised, is that I never believed them to work, so of course they didn't. Yet others who used these methods had outstanding results. The same applies when someone is taking what he or she believes is medicine when it is only a placebo; if you think it is going to work, it will.

People get fat by thinking fat thoughts. By seeing yourself fat you will always be fat. Whenever you try to lose weight, or anything else, it will always find you again. Instead of the negative connotation of losing weight, aim for your ideal weight.

Many who have weight control issues have the habit of comfort eating when they are under stress or feeling down. The problem with comfort eating is not so much the foods that are consumed at the time but the negative vibration surrounded with ingestion of the food. Those who comfort eat do so at times during low points. Just like those who take drugs or have alcohol issues, it is their way of dealing with an issue in their lives that they are not happy with. You will not come across too many people that are highly satisfied will all areas of their lives that have any of these problems. People resort to these cruxes as a way of trying to deal with a problem and it is an escape mechanism from their everyday life. Those that are eating from a place of negativity will always put on weight. Whenever you ingest food from a good feeling place it is almost impossible to gain weight.

Career

Do you feel that you work too many hours that you don't have time to do all the other things in life you enjoy? Are you working all week just to look forward to the weekend? Ask yourself why you keep persisting. If you cannot get up in the morning and feel inspired most of the time by what you are doing, why do you keep doing it? Many people don't mind taking money for something they hate doing, as it is a trade off. Many people feel guilty being paid for doing something that they enjoy, hence their reasons for not doing it. Don't allow yourself to fall into this category.

If this sounds like you then start being clear on what it is that you would like to do. Focus your thoughts on a job you will love, where you only have to work as many hours a week you would choose to with the level of pay you desire. You may have to make a small change to what it is you are doing, but in time, if you stay focused on your thoughts and go about your job in an appreciating mode until it turns up, it eventually has to happen. Any change that you do make will be to your liking as long as you put that intention forward. You may find someone mentions a vacancy to you in a job description you would not have given much thought to in the past, but upon thinking about it a bit more you start to see the benefits. Who knows what way it will turn up, just trust that it will.

You may be working in an industry that you have found is not to your liking and really don't know what it is that you want to do. Just ask yourself: what is it that would make you happy? Be open to the ideas and the ways they come about. I have not known all my life what I wanted to do. For over twenty years I went from job to job, not really liking any of them for any length of time. My attention span is short at the best of times, especially if I'm doing something I don't particularly enjoy or is repetitive. All my life I have never known what I truly wanted to do. Most kids knew what they wanted to be when they grew up, but I have never had any clue.

One day, when I had been wanting to know my purpose, I asked myself, 'What is it I love?' Not long after, a girlfriend of mine rang to say that she wanted me to take over her small gathering of people she had once a week to discuss spiritual topics. I had repeatedly told her no, as it was not the avenue I wanted to take. I enjoy the learning principles based on spirituality, but it would never be a career path I would want to follow. Then I instantly had a 'light bulb' moment. What I had been passionate about more than anything was the power of the mind and its connection to the universe and would love to tell people all about it. However, I thought just because it was a topic of interest to me, I was not sure whether others would grasp it as passionately. So I took on the group and incorporated a bit of her teachings with the bulk of mine. Each week, the group that came would say it is the highlight of the week and as you can see, has led me to writing this book and having regular forums on the subject.

You need to ask a clear question if you are unsure of the path you want to take. Ask yourself what is your passion that you could turn into a career path and bring with it a suitable income. Add to that question anything else you desire and then keep your mind open over the coming days, weeks, and months. Just don't focus too intently that you are repeling any desirable situations away from you.

What if you are stuck in a job you don't like but feel you have no other alternative? I understand this is a difficult situation as I have been in this predicament many times, so keep asking for what it is you desire. The answer will eventually come if you are open and eventually the right line of work will as well. The best thing you can do to the best of your ability is to go to work and enjoy your job, even if it means putting on a pretence. It is important to find some sort of fulfillment and be as co-operative as possible, as it is the only way to bring about new and improved conditions for you in the least amount of time. Focus on all enjoyable aspects about your job. By being resentful and difficult to work with, you are only prolonging the pain. Remember, the universe does not know the difference between you faking it and reality, but it does know when you are putting up resistance.

While working, keep thinking about what it is that you would like to do. Be welcoming and courteous to everyone around you. Once you start going to work with a new, improved attitude, the situations around you will get a little easier. Your constant attention to what it is that you want to do will eventually bring it to you. If you have difficult colleagues at work, read the chapter on *'Relationships'*. Ask yourself how is it you would like this person to treat you? Then focus on how you would like that to be. If you wish for them to be kinder to you and treat you with more respect, then think of that. If you think, "Oh, here they come, another criticism", then that is what you will get. Treat people how you like to be treated. It is very hard to be rude to someone who is being pleasant.

If you own your own business, give thought to the people you want to employ and at what level you wish for their involvement to be. Keep asking yourself and writing down the kind of employees and managers that you wish to hire. If you want someone who will take over some of your responsibilities so you can have more time off, factor that into the equation. If you want people to get on harmoniously, add that. When you are really sure of what it is you want, you will find that you will hire the right staff. Any wrong person for the job will be late, you will not be able to fit them in, you will miss their calls and them yours. Do not fight the resistance and push through. It is happening that way for a reason, because they are not right for the role. With the right people, everything will fall into place magically.

If you want your business to expand, think about that. If you want more customers, visualize them coming. Ask for ways to expand your business or how to increase your client base. Again, the right opportunities will present themselves, whether it is a different form of advertising or someone approaches you to amalgamate. Be open to what comes your way. The moment you concern yourself with any negativity you are allowing the possibility of that entering the equation. If you don't want it, don't focus on it.

You don't have to spend years getting a university degree to earn the money that will make you well off. Sure, if there is something that you have an interest in and would like to study, do it. If you want to study and have a job so money is coming in at the same time, ask for a job that will pay well around your study time. It will come as long as you believe it and let go of any resistance.

Don't think the only way you are going to make more money is by spending time studying to improve your qualifications, if that is not what you want. There are many great paying jobs that pay you to study and learn. There are many great paying jobs as well. Believe you deserve one of them and it will show up. Just keep enjoying what you are doing in the meantime until it does.

I was inspired by my desire for a lifestyle. Be the master of your own life.

Safety

B reak-ins, robberies, muggings and any other acts of crime can only happen if the person involved is in some way feeling vulnerable, insecure, threatened, or unsafe. You will find with any kind of incident to do with safety you have to feel unsafe, vunerable or believe it could happen to you in the first place. As stated at the start of the book, some concepts may be hard for you to comprehend. I am aware that this is most difficult for many to believe, that these atrocities are not some random event, but if you can talk to anyone who has had an unfortunate incident in their lives and work out their emotions or thought patterns leading up to the event, you will gain a better understanding.

Often I leave my handbag and computer unattended in a public place or my car and house unlocked, which I'm sure most would think is irresponsible, but I know the rules, and no harm can come to me when I truly trust. If fact, at the time of me writing this a home invasion took place in our street two days before and this has not changed my attitude in any way. Anyone in my vicinity that may be half-tempted would either be distracted, caught, or contemplate the situation a little too long that it just does not occur.

My own belief started around this a few years ago before I became aware of these universal laws. At the time, I was working at a club in an area renowned for drugs, theft, and crime. My central locking was not working, so I left my car unlocked and trusted my car was safe and protected. This is something I was taught while I was on my spiritual journey, and to say thank you in advance; however, I didn't truly believe in it at the time until this incident. Apparently, someone was looking through all the cars in the car park to see if any were easily accessible. The cellar man, who just happened to be walking past the front door to go on a break (the club had not yet opened at the time, so there wasn't a flow of patrons in and out of the club), had seen this suspicious person just as he had reached my car. The timing of him walking past the door just as this man approached my car seemed serendipitous, and by far more than a coincidence that left me totally astonished, but now I know that is how life works.

As long as you feel protected and safe you are. You can use this technique on anyone or anything. If you feel unsafe, ask for safety. If you are walking home in the dark or are taking a train, ask to be protected during your journey and you will find you will be guided to the right situation or carriage where you will be safe. A friend told me of a time when she was a little girl, she had been enticed to a quiet location by a man with the intention of molesting her. Before any serious consequence took place, she was aware she was in a very dire situation and said to herself, 'Someone please help me.' Within a split second someone came walking down the stairs, distracting the man, and he ran away. She didn't even have to say it out loud for her call to be heard. You just have to ask.

I know all parents are concerned for their child's safety; but pointing out to them what could happen all the time will in fact increase the likelihood of a potentially harmful situation surrounding their loved one. The reason is if your children feel unsafe or vulnerable, your constant worry about it raises their vibration for it to happen. Always tell your children if they are in a position where they feel vulnerable to ask for safety and protection. As crazy as it sounds it works, and wouldn't you rather they always be protected, even if you don't understand the principles behind it? I know it seems like a double-edged sword; if you don't point the dangers out to them and something happens, you will never forgive yourself. Of course, teach them how to stay safe, but don't drill them incessantly with the possibilities of something bad always happening to them. They will never come to a place of trusting anyone and will be wary that everyone has an ulterior motive. You can only attract untrusting situations into your life if you lack trust.

When I am in my car, I always drive with the intention of being safe and accident free. I always see my son being safe. If he is out at night, I always trust he is safe, and if I start to have any doubt, I say to myself, 'thank you for keeping him safe'. I almost always feel safe, but if I am home by myself, or I feel otherwise, I ask to be kept safe.

You will find the people who are attacked or injured are those who are feeling vulnerable, victimized, negative and/or angry. They are the ones being hurt, raped, murdered, injured or are sick. People who are angry draw other angry people and situations to them. However, an innocent person can draw these awful situations to them, if they think it can happen to them and are feeling vulnerable.

My son went through a bit of a dark period not too long ago. He had been out of work for a while and was spending too much time alone, which can lead to many unwanted thoughts. He has never been a child I had to worry about getting into fights or doing something deemed reckless. He was always sensible and thought of the consequence of being hurt before he delved into any situation. However, in the space of a few weeks, he had two very out-of-character altercations. The first came on New Year's Day when he met a couple of friends at a hotel. Being on his provisional license, he was only able to drink soft drink, so he was sober at the time. Yet a person he did not know came up and head butted him out of the blue.

A few weeks later, he was celebrating a public holiday with friends at one of their houses. He had slipped over the edge of the driveway into a ditch several meters below, only inches from a metal pole that was protruding out of the ground and broke a few ribs. Looking back to that day, I said to him in the afternoon that I did not want him to attend the party. It is quite possible that my concern had a bearing on the night's events. Even though he does not agree, I have no doubt both of these incidences were drawn to him because of his state of mind, and possibly mine.

If you think bad things will happen to you, in time they will.

Relationships

I have left the subject of relationships as one of the last topics to discuss as it is the most difficult for many to comprehend, that you can help change someone else's behavior by simply changing your own thoughts about them. Hopefully, you have grasped some of the content already presented to you in this book, so you have a firmer foundation to understand the power behind this information.

Quite often, someone enters into a relationship because they are trying to escape either their parents or another relationship that has not been serving them, particularly if their upbringing had a negative impact on them. When this happens, they have not given themselves enough time to think about what they truly want in a partner, they are so eager to escape whatever it is they are running from to fill that void. Because of this, they tend to gravitate towards what it is they just left as they have not had enough time to rid the old pattern from their system, hence attracting more of the same. I am sure you know people who have left one relationship only to wind up with one similar to the last, or someone who has left home prematurely only to be in a relationship that is not bringing them happiness. They may think to themselves that when they entered into this relationship they were not aware what the person was like when they first met them and then their partner changed, so how were they supposed to know? That is true, of course someone is not going to show their negative side until they are comfortable in the relationship, however what drew the two together unconsciously in the first place was the invisible signals they were giving off. Because they were offering a similar frequency, the universe draws them together and even though it did not seem like that at the time, they got what they were offering vibrationally. It was just in disguise.

If you have been in a similar situation, before this happens again, give more thought to what you would like in your new partner. Through the process of law of attraction you can control the circumstances surrounding you by your thoughts and your feelings, not your actions, and you attract to you the people and circumstances you desire. Do not wind up creating by default because you have not been clear enough with your wishes in a partner.

Before you enter into another relationship take all the negative aspects from your previous ones, turn them into a positive statement, and then only focus on that. It may mean waiting a little longer for the right person to come to you, but wouldn't you rather wait and be with the right person than spending years with the wrong one again? Unfortunately, many would rather jump into another relationship that does not serve them as the alternative to being alone for that period of time. This is where a major problem occurs as you expect someone else to make you happy instead of finding your own happiness, and you will keep repeating the same patterns until you learn to break them. If your happiness depends on another, you will never be truly free.

The trick is take your attention off the person's behavior that you do not like as focusing on their negatives will only bring more of them into reality. Chances are, once you stop pointing out how inappropriate their behavior is, they will stop acting that way and will then behave more in a way that you desire. If by chance they choose not to stop the behavior, it is highly likely that in time the relationship will run its course and make way for someone who is more in tune with your desires. But when you keep focusing on the negatives and they focus on yours, it is that resistance that is holding you together through the negative aspects you are both pointing out to one another.

When you are in a relationship already, it is mentally tougher to follow this process, as many of the habits have been there a long time, more than likely before you were even together, so you have been tolerating them for a while. You may even think that the problem belongs to them and not you, so why should you make the effort? They are probably thinking that they have been like that from the start, and you should accept them for who they are instead of trying to get them to change so late into the relationship. You probably have thoughts that if they loved you enough, they wouldn't do the things that hurt or annoy you. You may be thinking, 'Why am I the one having to do all this work when they are the one with the problem?' In principle you are right however, that is not going to fix the problem. You have a few choices: to leave and find someone else you are more compatible with, (in which case you are more than likely going to attract a similar situation again), think your way to your partner improving, or stay and tolerate the way it is now.

If you are not happy you have to ask yourself whether you really want to stay or whether your partner is worth expending this energy for. That is up to you to decide. I know it is hard to think positive thoughts when the behavior they have been offering may have been happening for a very long time, but ask yourself, is the way you are currently dealing with it working? If not, and you're not happy, you need to make some sort of change. I don't think that anyone should tolerate any behavior that he or she strongly disapproves of, but by pointing out their behavior or habits to them in a negative way will only make the situation worse. Think of a time when someone told you what you were doing was inappropriate. It didn't feel good, did it? You probably kept doing it just to show them or make your point. There is probably a tug of war going on, a battle for control. Someone needs to make the first move, so if you think the relationship is worth keeping, it may be up to you.

If you decide they are worth the effort, think of them in the manner you would like them to be and more importantly, focus on the good qualities they do have, not the bad ones. See them exactly the way you intend them to be. If they drink too much, see them sober; if they are not working, see them employed and happy. If they don't help enough around the house, see them being helpful and appreciate their effort. Keep telling them they are useless and that is how they will be. Keep holding grudges or resentment and they will stay the same. Do not react to their present behavior, which will only cause you and them to go backwards. Even if their behavior does not change overnight, and it probably won't, it will eventually have an impact. Only after a while can you decide whether the impact it has had is enough for you to want to stay. Most times, the impact is enough to change things for the better. What you will find is, if you have been doing this process effectively and not speaking or thinking about the behavior that annoys you, is that your partner will over time start acting in the way you desire.

If you give your attention to what it is you don't like, it will manifest itself more into the experience. The behavior may stop temporarily; however, what you will find is that the relationship goes back to its old habits and patterns after a while, even if counseling is sought. If the behavior has been put to rest, it most often means that they may be pushing that aspect of themselves down to make their partner happy, but in turn they are making a sacrifice that does not make them happy, by having to alter their behavior for someone else. People cannot change unless they really want to, not because it will make the partner happy. It could be much better to let go of this relationship so both can find someone who is more compatible with each partner. It would be better for both to be able to be themselves in a different relationship than changing themselves to stay in one that does not suit them. The behavior should change only if they really do wish to alter it because it will be beneficial for them, not just their partner. This includes anything harmful, such as addictions, abuse, and the like. You only ever have full control over yourself, how you behave, and how you react at any given time. So the way you react to what they are doing is going to have the greatest impact.

A person may willingly give up a hobby or part of their life if it is not going to be missed. Such as, if you really enjoy a sport but all your nights are taken up with work or other activities and you are happy to give up sport because you would rather your relationship, that's up to you. However, if you give up all your activities to satisfy a clingy partner, ask yourself what would you rather have: no life and a clingy partner or a different partner who will allow you some of your own time and a happy relationship? The choice is always yours, and of course, some topics of contention are bigger than this.

When you wish to change someone's behavior, first you have to ask yourself why? If it is because you find their behavior dangerous or detrimental, they are certainly good reasons. If there are a few things that could be improved upon, fine. However, if any of the reasons are due to your own insecurity, jealousy, or unhappiness, you may be directing your attention to the wrong person. Many think that by changing their partner they will be happy; however, they are only going to find something else to complain about, as there is an aspect in their own life they are not happy with. Most annoyances you find in another are a mirror of your own issues.

Hold your loved ones in high esteem. That way
you will always bring out the best in them.

If you are not in a relationship, give thought to the qualities you would like in a partner. The good thing about not-so-good relationships is that it helps to define what it is that you do want. If you had a partner who was unreliable, you may desire one who is dependable. If your previous partner was inconsiderate, thoughtless, lazy, and messy, did not have the same interests, gambled, drank too much, smoked, or was unfaithful, it gives you more clarity to what you want next. The first thing to do is to appreciate any past relationships. Do not hold onto any hurts or hang-ups. Appreciate them for what they were. Appreciate the aspects that you enjoyed and eliminate the ones you didn't, and then you will be clearer about what you want. Remember, that person appeared in your life for a reason, which was to help you to grow in an area of your life.

If you want a partner that will be faithful and loyal, the universe will deliver that to you. Remember, what you think about you get, whether you want it or not. Do not think of an unfaithful partner if you do not desire one. Think of a faithful one. You will find that you will not come across the wrong kind of person for you if you are focused on what it is you want. It is law; it cannot be any other way. Think of only what you want, and the universe will bring you like-minded people; stop mixing your thoughts up with somebody else's. You will start to realize you are actually doing the other person a favor by being selfish and only focusing on your own desires. That way, you will be matched up with someone who has the same desires as you. If you think of other people's desires that is when you both do not get what it is you want.

If you have children from a previous relationship, you may ask for a partner who will be supportive, kind to your children, and have a great relationship with them. If you worry about finding those aspects in a partner, then the universe will not bring the right person to you. It is really important to focus on what you want and leave out what you don't; then there can be no mistake. You cannot get what you don't want as long as you have not put it out there by default. Trust that the right person will come.

Once you have asked for the kind of partner that you desire, you do not have to worry about winding up with the wrong one unless you become impatient and try to make something happen before it is ready, then you will not get what it is you want. You will find any not-so-suitable partnerships will not get off the ground. When you make a date with someone who is not suitable, a series of events will take place to make the meeting difficult. You will find that their or your car will break down on the way, one of you will get sick or you will have to make alternate plans, or you will miss each other's calls. These are all very strong signs that this is not the right person; so if you constantly try to push through these inconveniences on purpose, you will end up with the wrong person. Getting together with the right one should be easy.

This technique works on any relationship, including difficult co-workers, children, parents, and siblings. I recall having a difficult co worker who everyone complained about. Instead of getting on the bandwagon like everyone else, I simply went about my job and ignored the problem. Not too long after the co-worker was sacked. Once you change the way you view people in your life and stop reacting to their behavior, they will either start acting in the way you wish, or they will be not have as much of an impact on you. My son, being a normal young man, at times drinks more alcohol than I would like him to. On occasion I have voiced my disapproval to him, only to be confronted with more of this unwanted behavior. I do have to accept that he is the dictator of his own life, but when I focus on him being the person I desire him to be, that is drinking less, as soon as I stop judging him and condemning his behavior, he does becomes a much more responsible drinker.

Another time around the same issue, I woke during the night

noticing he was not yet home. I was a little concerned as I knew he had an engagement early in the morning where he would be driving, and being on his provisional license, he could not afford to have alcohol in his system. I stopped my thoughts, knowing this is my son's life and that he is a sensible young man, he will work it out and then went back to sleep. Not long after he came home and woke me up, and asked if I could give him a lift in the morning as he was aware the alcohol would still be present in his body. Did my thought process have a direct influence on his or was it just a coincidence? It doesn't really matter as long as the desired outcome took place.

Focus on all your relationships on how you want them to be. Before you come into contact with someone, spend a little quiet time to yourself. Give your attention to the best aspects of that person and visualize them how you wish them to be. When you eventually come into contact, your vibration around them will have changed, which in turn will help them to soften as they will have either consciously or unconsciously become aware of this. When you get your back up about anything, the automatic response is to go on the defense, and this is what you want to avoid. Remember, like attracts like; so you cannot attract people into your vicinity unless you have a matching response to theirs. Volatile people attract other volatile people and so on.

You may wonder why it is that opposites seem to attract and feel this may be contradictory to what it is we have been focusing on. How is it that couples that seem so different are drawn together? This occurs when one partner is looking to another partner to bring out a trait in them that they don't have but would really desire. An example of this is a very quiet natured person may have drawn to themselves a loud and outgoing person. This has come about as that person has always wanted to be more outgoing, and they focus on that missing aspect, drawing that kind of person into their experience. You may also wonder, how can a timid person attract someone aggressive? If you are concerned with being hurt or intimidated, it is then highly likely it will occur. You will find that if you abhor a certain type of person or behavior, often they are the ones drawn into your life quicker. Anything you resent turns up in your life as a learning tool. As the saying goes, *what you resist persists.*

People's opinions and desires are not always going to be in alignment with yours. Respect theirs, just like you would want them to respect yours. That does not mean you have to accept their thinking, just let them be. They are on a different wavelength to yours. If it bothers you, it's best not to spend too much time in their company or you will simply attract more of it into your life if you keep on focusing on it.

Tips and Techniques

Do you spend a good deal of time having useless random thoughts that have no bearing on your life? Become aware of this and alter them to your advantage. The instant you recognize them, replace them with more constructive thoughts that will have a positive impact on your future. It is the small everyday thoughts that are causing you the biggest problems. Clean up all those small damaging thoughts and start to see the difference in your life.

It is best to only focus on one or two desires to start with. When you have too many your focus becomes scattered which splits your energy by dividing it into too many areas, leading to confusion. Often your thoughts need enough power behind them for them to eventually come to fruition. It is too hard to give your attention to too many things at once. When those things have been achieved and you are getting the hang of it, work on the next subjects you wish to seek improvement on. If you are capable of focusing on more than two at a time without getting flustered, then go right ahead. However, stop and concentrate on less if it becomes a problem. That does not mean you cannot focus on the positives of all situations; this is something you need to train yourself to do constantly.

As mentioned, thoughts most of the time need some sort of power behind them to be able to eventuate into reality. It is highly unlikely a random thought will surface into reality; however, occasionally this can happen. One Friday morning while cleaning the bathroom, I gave my attention to the shower head I should replace, as it was a fixed head that was not adjustable. That afternoon a gentleman knocked on my door to inform me he was installing complimentary water-saving shower heads, and the very one he had was the adjustable model I pictured. I had a thought that someone in close proximity was a match to. I marvel each and every time I have one of these experiences.

You only have now, find any way you can to enjoy it.

Always look at the benefit of your desire, instead of the negative of not having it. If you think of wanting a relationship because you are bored, that it is better than being by yourself, you will not attract the right partner. However, thinking they will be fun to be with and it would be nice to share some like-minded company and you will enhance each other's lives, these are good reasons for your thoughts.

Visualizing is the most powerful method to activating your vibration and to bring to you what it is you desire. Spend time doing this, even if it's only for a short period of time, you will gain the benefits. Sit or lie down, and ensure you will not be interrupted. Play some calming music if you wish. Start as you would a meditation. Just quiet your mind and relax. Start to think of your ideal life. The desires you have. How you want your partner and/or children to be. What would make your life better for you? It can be anything you want: a partner, job, house, car, more holidays, better health. Feel the excitement, the feelings of happiness and contentment stirring within you. If you only have five or ten minutes, that's fine. Just try and do it as often as possible when you have a little alone time—in the car, on the train, while you are doing something that does not require your attention. Once you start, you will find it easier and easier and you should look forward to this time. The purpose of this exercise is to also train yourself to think this is your new life now. It will become second nature and the law of attraction will start bringing you opportunities to live it. This is no different to what professional athletes do to bring about their successes.

Live what it is you are asking. You may feel like you are telling yourself a little lie but it is only a short-term one as it will be on its way to you soon. If you keep looking at everything as it is in its present form, then that is all it will ever be. Wimbledon champions dreamt from the time they were a small child they would be standing on centre court holding that trophy. It's the desire to have it that put them there, the dreaming. Start dreaming your ideal life into existence.

When you desire something or need an answer, ask clearly. Think about what you want and then put it to the universe clearly. Muddled questions will only bring muddled answers. If you want a clear answer, ask a clear question. Such as, instead of saying "How can I find the right job, I don't know where to look," say, "Lead me to a line of work would I be most passionate about." Even if you don't know what it is that you wish to do, situations and thoughts will come to you to help clarify your desires. Or make a statement. "I know I will find a job I enjoy that is local and pays well." Of course, change it to anything you desire. Understand the reason why you may be getting a mixed bag. You need to be clearer in your asking.

Once you have asked trust, do not try and work out where it will come from as you will limit your possibilities. If you say it will only come one way, then that is all you are allowing. Sure, be clear enough to know what you want but not too clear that you start to feel worried instead of positive. It is always all about feeling good, not anxious or worrisome.

Simply focus on the end result and not the pathway to your goal. You do not need to know all the details of how to get there. How could you know when you have not been there before? That way you will attract the right avenue for you again as long as are you don't worry.

Stop concerning yourself with what others think that could have you doubting yourself and instead start to live your life as if your desire is already in existence. No matter what it is, 'trick' yourself in to believing it. If you have any doubt about your worthiness or ability to achieve your goal, or are worried about what others think, it cannot eventuate.

When you put out a desire through your thoughts, it should eventually be able to find its way to you quite easily, or you should not have to look too far to find it. If doors keep closing on you or you find the process quite arduous, you are trying too hard and are in fact turning it away. Maybe the timing is not right. Trust; when it is, it will appear without hardly any effort on your part.

Do not counteract your positive thoughts with a negative one. Every time you think of something you want but then add a reason why it can't happen, you have counteracted it. Every time you point out why it isn't in your existence yet you have counteracted it. If you have more positive than negative thoughts, it will eventually turn up. If you have all positive and no negative thoughts, it will turn up a lot quicker.

If something is happening in your life that you don't like, stop giving it your attention. Stop talking and thinking about it. Just think about that which gives you pleasure. This can be very hard to do at first. You are so used to thinking the way you do that you have trained your mind, so you do need to retrain it. The law of attraction brings one negative thought then another. Once you think a different way, one positive thought will bring another and yet another. When you do slip and have a negative thought, you will be very aware of it and be able to rectify the problem much sooner. For now, this will be your most constant battle. If you have things in your life you like, keep talking and thinking about them and appreciating them. The same goes for the things that you want that have not appeared yet. Trust that they will as long as you are giving positive energy to it.

Appreciation is a very big key to getting what you desire quicker. Appreciate where you are today. Appreciate what is around you no matter how bad things are, for all you have is now. Chances are you cannot change your present surrounding that you are in this instant. It is all you have in this moment, so you need to love it. You need to find a way to be happy, to accept your present circumstances; otherwise you will only attract more of the same. Know that if you can find a positive thought, more will keep coming until your life improves. If you are looking where you are at and are not happy, you are telling the universe through your vibration you don't believe things can change.

Saying thank you in advance means you trust it will all work out before you even start to see any evidence of it. Be thankful in advance that you are going to get it, whether it's a parking space, a job promotion or anything else for that matter.

When you start to worry about anything, you allow the possibility of what it is that you are concerned about to become a reality.

When you have a desire for anything, you only need to ask once; but most of the time you do need to give it some extra thought so it can appear. You need to activate the vibration in you for it to show. Think about your desire and feel it into your life. At times only a simple thought is needed. A perfect example of this is when you think of someone and you bump into them or they ring you. Your vibration matched up to theirs, and that is how they appear. You both had to be in a close mental frequency for this to happen.

Upon waking in the morning, spend a few minutes in bed and give thought to how you wish your day to be. Plan it in your mind ahead of time. Again, give appreciation for all that you are grateful for and think of having a great day. In addition, if you have time, think of your desires, and spend a little time thinking as if you are living them now. Get into the habit of feeling like this often.

Whatever you think about in the now is your dominant thought. So if you think you can, then that's most dominant. If you think you can't, that is most dominant. Whatever you think is your perception of reality, not what the actual reality is. So change your perception of reality to what you want it to be.

Before you undertake any task, especially if it is one that you feel anxious about or don't particularly enjoy, spend a few minutes feeling good about it and focus on the outcome you wish to achieve. Think of all the benefits that will be gained and then forge ahead, remembering to let go of any resistance and not holding on too tightly to the outcome.

Whatever it is you want will only come to you from a place of wholeness, not a place of absence. If you focus on the negative reason why you want something, then it won't come. An example is: if you want a job that pays more money, do not focus on the fact that you do not have enough money to pay your bills or that you don't like your job, which will only keep it from you. Turn it around and look for the positives. You would like more money as it will allow you more opportunities and freedom. You would like a new job as it will expand your mind. You always have to come from place of appreciation. It does not matter how bad things are, you can always focus on a positive aspect. Whenever you feel something is missing from your life, it will not come to you.

Live your life as if you already have your requests. That way, you are 'tricking' the universe. Quite often, things come to you that you don't really need much more easily than those that you do because you do not have resistance to those other factors. You also only ever have to ask once; however, thinking about it will make it feel more real, especially if this something that you don't feel ready for. Remember, your desires have to match a vibration to what it is you are asking for, and if you don't feel worthy of it, it can't happen. The more you think and feel yourself living with your desire; it will eventually line up and come to you.

If the thing you want is causing you pain by not having it, you are not ready to receive it.

When you desire something but don't believe you will get it, your doubt is suppressing your strong signal to the universe.

If you think you have to beat somebody or win at all costs to have it, you are not in a mode to receive it.

You cannot think about something once; say it's useless and give up, and still expect it to come to you. But if you have had a strong desire for a while, then give up (all you are doing is letting go of the angst surrounding it; you aren't actually giving up) it will then come along. This happens because you have let go of the resistance. If something you have wanted for a long time is still yet to appear in your life it means you have resistance, an attachment to the outcome. If it hurts to not have it, if thinking about it makes you feel anxious, if your breathing changes you have resistance. If this has been happening for a while, the best thing to do now is let go. It is okay to feel sad, to tell yourself it is not going to happen. Almost always when you give up like this and let go of the expectation the very thing will pop into your life not too long after but you must truly let go and stop looking.

No amount of prayer by way of bargaining, pleading, begging etc. will bring forth your desire. Higher power can sense your desperation and until you can learn to live without your wish, your dream will never come to fruition. Surrendering to the unknown is the only solution in this case.

The most important part of this whole process that I cannot stress enough is coming to a place of acceptance, where you are allowing your desires to flow to you. Sometimes you think you have come to that place but chances are you haven't; however, you can't see that at the time. If at any time you are wondering 'where is it?', and you feel disappointed it hasn't happened yet, then you haven't. When you think like that, change your motto to, 'I know it will come when the time is right'. That way you are softening your thoughts and letting go of any resistance which is preventing your request.

If thinking about what you want makes you feel anxious, stop! You are now having resistance, an attachment to the outcome. You have to let go of this thing you want and look to revisit it down the track only if you can let go of the worry. I had to do the same very thing with this book. A few years ago I was so desperate to make it a success and get this information out there it was the only thing I thought about and was destroying my life. I realized one day I could pick it up and not worry if it was a success or not, that is when everything fell into place.

The reason why people think they are not resistant when they are is because they are under stress in their life and have probably been resistant for a very long time. They have gotten used to the tension they arc under and it feels normal to them, however, it's not.

If you think you can, you will. If you think you can't, you won't. The reason for this is by believing that you can, the universe will open up the opportunities for you to be able to act. However, if you think otherwise, the divine intelligence will close down any possibility for you to be able to achieve whatever it is that you have asked for.

> *Your job is to know the question; the answer*
> *will come with the right question.*

Once you have asked, let go, your work is done. It is the universes' job to match your desire and work out its way to you, not yours. It will put the deal together for you, so go about your life as normal and be open to the possibilities that are about to come your way.

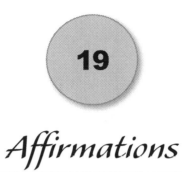

Affirmations

In the past, I had never been a fan of affirmations. To me they seemed like a wishy-washy way to try and believe something that was unbelievable. However, affirmations are a great way to get you to a place of accepting and mentally preparing yourself in a positive mindset, so they are very useful. Now I know the way we perceive anything has the biggest impact in achieving them; affirmations have a purpose in that they train your mind into believing the possibilities.

The purpose of an affirmation is to say, whatever it is, over and over again, until you feel comfortable with the new-found belief or thought, so it resonates through you and eventually the constant repetitiveness will sink into your sub-conscious. Let's say you don't feel comfortable around money. But now you know the only way to allow money in is to improve your relationship with it and start to be more comfortable with it. By stating to yourself over and over, money comes to you easily, you will get to a place where you will start to really believe it, and once you do, money will start flowing. Of course, you can use an affirmation around any subject you like. You do not have to use someone else's; you can make your own. Say it to yourself over and over again. Once you start believing it and seeing evidence, you know it is working.

Quotes and other sayings, even ones that you make up yourself have just as much impact as well. Find a few that you find really inspiring and leave them in places where you can see them on a regular basis. Make an effort every day to focus on them and feel good about the outcome.

20

Signs and How to Recognize Them

People have often been told to follow their intuition however, ninety percent of the time intuition is overruled by emotion and ego due to uncertainty. Whenever you are emotionally charged regarding an issue it is very hard to tell the difference between intuition, emotion or ego. That is when following signs is the best path you can take. When you have asked for something, the right path will open up and the wrong one will have many obstacles in the way. As long as you trust, you will get what it is you want.

People tend to get a sign and dismiss it as they are not trusting, do not know how to read them, or don't believe them to be true, yet if you can alter this belief, they are very useful. Learn to recognize your signs. They are there to help you head in the direction you are choosing. They will only be confusing if you have doubt about them and believe them to be.

When you ask for something in your life, trust it will be brought to you the right way. If you have asked for help in losing weight and you happen to be introduced to a dietitian, this is not by accident. A friend was looking for a new job in her chosen field and then met a supervisor through a friend of a rival company. These happened for a reason; you have summoned the event into your life. You need to learn to be open and read the signs; the same with any other event or circumstance.

I find that if I am having a thought that I shouldn't be or if it doesn't support the direction I am heading in, I am interrupted either by the phone or some other means. This happens all the time. At first, I wasn't aware of this, but after a while I caught on to the pattern. I am able to read these signs very well as I have already gotten my life to a place of minimum disruption. If your life is chaotic, you may need to gain more control if you wish to try this technique, as it may be confusing for you. However, you may be aware if an interruption is for a good reason.

One time, I was writing on a birthday card and the phone rang. I could not believe it as I was only writing on a card, and this call made me have my doubts about this sign. I did not pick up; I continued to write on the card and then listen to the message. The call was from the birthday girl, saying she was not able to make our gathering and that I would not see her for a month. Another time I was in the queue of a supermarket buying a microwave. Just as I approached the check out my phone rang which was quite inconvenient timing. I got the microwave home only to have it not fit into the allocated space. I never doubted this sign again after these and many more incidents.

*Focus only on what you want; anything
more will get in your way.*

The same thing happens when I am making a purchase that is not suitable, whether it is on the Internet or at the shops. I would often be interrupted when buying a pair of shoes. I used to get annoyed by this, only to get them home, walk in them for a while, and realize they were most uncomfortable. When making a purchase off the net that is not right, similar things happen, the computer plays up, and the screen will go blank or drop out. These are particular signs I have asked for when I am choosing incorrectly, to be interrupted. You can ask for any kind of sign you wish for as well. This could also occur with response to people or a job application. I have learnt not to override the signs. If I continually miss a call for a job interview or am interrupted, it's not the right job.

I took a friend with me to test drive a few cars as I was thinking of updating mine. When we were about to take a car for a ride, my phone rang. It had not rung all morning. When I told her the car was not the right one, and the reason I believed it to be so, she told me I read too much into signs. When it happened another two times that day, one after the other, she did not know what to make of it. I don't think the incidents totally convinced her; however, I do think it made her take notice.

If my interruptions are of a positive nature, such as I have been waiting to hear a positive outcome to a situation or some other good news, I am aware that the interruption is to let me know all is fine and am I on the right track. However, if it is a random disturbance something is either telling me to stop, wait or turn around.

Everything does fall into place when the timing is right. It does work that way with divine timing, usually three or four things will fall into place at once. You may have waited months, even longer for them, but there they are, all lined up in a very short span of time. I think there are a few reasons for this. You have gotten yourself in a much better place of receiving and everything lines up perfectly. I also believe the universe wants us to know that there is something working with us, and by doing this it is making us pay attention.

View the universe as being an overhead projector; it can see everything that is happening in your life—your thoughts and what it is you have asked for, your next moves and also those of the people you are about to interact with. You can only see your immediate surroundings; you do not have the same foresight, hence why we feel uncertain and wary. The higher power has heard your call and is now in the process of putting all the bits and pieces together for you, even though you can't see it. You just have to ask, relax and trust it will be set up to your liking as long as you do not allow any doubt or fear to enter the equation. Trust you are going to get there and it is all being worked out for you; you just have to be open to it and keep going in the right direction.

This is where many people start to lose faith and wonder 'where is it?' and often do not receive what it is they are after as they believe it is not coming, or they think they have asked incorrectly, so they change direction. When you do this you are confusing the universe and it may bring you a mixture of what it is you're after, or put it on hold until you are in back on track again. It is important at this point to be patient. Do not try and force the situation and make it happen before it's time to be delivered to you.

Let's say you are sending out a signal for a certain kind of partner (who you don't yet know), but there are two problems; one is that this particular person is currently living in another state and the other is that they are partnered up with someone else (albeit unhappily). The universe has heard your call and has started the process of getting them to you. Next, the partner of the person you will wind up with has a job transfer to your city. Their partner (yours in the making) has decided to come with them for a new start. Once they make it there, they break up. A short time later, they somehow run into you (don't worry, it will happen), and bingo, you think it was all an accident. But that is not the case, and it was all pre-arranged; you simply could not see all the behind-the-scenes work that needed to be done to get them to you.

When I was in the third week of selling my house myself, I still did not have an offer that I was happy with. My girlfriend rang and asked if I wanted to go to an all-day event in the city the following week. My first thought was that I would be having an open home that Saturday, but my trusting mind knew otherwise. I told her I would go as I knew the universe would know more about what was happening in my life than I did; maybe it could see a buyer out there ready to make an offer that I didn't yet know about. Three hours later, that is exactly what happened and I was then free the following week.

A few days later, the pest and building inspector rang to book an inspection on behalf of the buyers. The time he requested, I had a friend coming over for lunch, so I put him off until the following day. I didn't want my friend around at that time of the inspection as he, unlike me, is a bit of pessimist. I hadn't even told him I was selling my home or writing a book. He would think this is all nonsense and ask why I would be selling when I had not organized where I would be moving to. I didn't want to be under his scrutiny, so the best thing was to change the time. My friend rang that night to say he couldn't come to lunch but instead would be over later that afternoon. I really should have known better, known the universe could see something I couldn't.

Everything always works out for me because I ask for it to be that way. I am hardly ever double-booked as I expect everything to slot together perfectly; when on the odd occasion I am, it is almost always because the second event is one that I would not wish to attend, so I have to politely decline. I can simply apologize and say I have something else on. Other times, something that I was attending had been cancelled only to have something else of greater interest take its place. Some people get flustered when things like this happen, but they haven't learnt to understand it happens this way for a reason; instead, they get caught up with the indecision whereas if they trusted, they would realize the decision has already been made for them. If a plan is meant to be changed and is for good reason, it will change without me having to interfere.

When you offer a thought and are waiting for the materialization to occur in your life, you will start to see evidence of it around you. You will see it show up in friends and other people you meet; you will get some of what you want but not the whole during this time. It is really important that while this is happening to see it as positive signs and to be happy for those who are benefiting, not that the universe is teasing you and leaving you out (even though it may feel like it). Remember that you have asked the universe for something and it is trying to show you it's on the way by bringing such circumstances to you. This is not to rub it in your face and show you what you are missing out on. It's to show you to have faith and your time will come. However, it is most important to not get too excited as this sense of hope can lead to attachment, putting back the desired outcome.

When you keep missing out on jobs you have applied for, it means that the right position has not come about for you yet; the interviews are practice for you to perfect them and feel comfortable in front of your future employer when the right job does show up. I kept looking for a home and had a long list of attributes that I thought may be a little unrealistic. Each time I would walk into a home it would have one that the previous house didn't have but would lack in another. Just at the time I sold my house, the one with everything I wanted turned up. It may have been a little frustrating at first, but the universe knew what it was that I was asking for and was just getting the setting right so it all fell into place.

Think your way to a better future.

Remember, if anything is hard, if you keep missing phone calls, if doors keep closing on you, it means that is not the right avenue for you to take or the time is not right, (that's assuming that you are not stopping the flow of your opportunity due to resistance). Let's say you are going for a job and you keep missing the calls for the interview and everything around it seems hard, it means it is not the right job for you. Keep persisting and you will wind up in the wrong job. A friend was bidding on a house at auction, and just as they got to the lot they were about to bid on, a siren went off and the rooms had to be evacuated. The following week they bought the right home for them. Everything happens for a reason.

This particular day I had a free morning, and being a beautiful summer's day I thought I would spend a little time down at the beach. I drove around for nearly fifteen minutes trying to find a parking space, which is most unusual. During that time I had missed a call from a friend. After calling her back, the call had a very negative connotation that was quite unsettling. After thinking about it for a while, I realized that I should not have called back, because if I was meant to hear the call and heed the message, it would have happened when it was a convenient time. It made me aware of the reason why it took me so long to park my car, so I would miss the call. After putting it all together, the call did not bother me anymore.

Four months before Christmas a few friends were discussing my dog Cooper's health, saying that he was tired and ready to depart. I found this a little hard to believe as he still seemed to have a lot of life left in him. Feeling sad, I picked him up and asked him if he would stay until Christmas, thinking he would be around much longer than this. Christmas morning came and I had to take him to the vet as he was not himself and the doctor advised that Cooper should be put down. I had forgotten about the above conversation until the day arrived and was upset I wasn't more specific with my words.

That afternoon I gave a friend a book that I originally bought for her as a house warming gift about 6 weeks before, however, for some reason I decided it was more appropriate for Christmas. When she opened the present we all gasped as the title of the book (as I had forgotten) was *All Pets Go To Heaven*. My son and I felt immense comfort knowing this was a sign. I was baffled as to what had made me change my mind and keep it for Christmas instead of for the house warming even though being an avid pet lover; she would have greatly appreciated it. It goes to show we have little whispers in our ear we are totally oblivious to.

I will close this chapter with one other story. A month before Christmas I had experienced something that I had never done so before. I had heard of it and mentioned it earlier in the book but never sensed this myself. Cooper went on medication for a heart murmur as he was having difficulty breathing. The vet assured me it was treatable and he would be fine with medication. However, every time his breathing was a little erratic I would panic and I would rush him to the vet, including a few times at night. Each time the vet said he was fine. I felt frustrated in being inconvenienced and not being aware if he was sick or not. I asked for a sign for me to know when he is struggling.

A few days later I woke not being able to breathe properly; my breathing had become very shallow. I was also experiencing intense discomfort in my abdominal area, and my stomach had ballooned to twice its size, conditions I have never had before. This went on for hours until I thought of Cooper. I wondered if I was taking on his pain, since I had asked to know when he was unwell. Once I had that thought, I took him to the vet and they put him on another medication and my discomfort subsided. To me this was truly miraculous as this was the first time I had ever had such an understanding of this, and it gave me tremendous insight into what general practitioners experience when they get too emotionally involved in their patients conditions. It made me realize why doctors can seem somewhat detached from their patients; it is a defense mechanism saving them from the same fate.

Setting the Intention

You can intend to have or be anything you desire in your life, as long as you are a vibrational match, it will come. You just have to go about asking the right way so you get exactly what it is you want. You do not always need to ask as the vibration you are offering will dictate what it is you desire. An example of this is that I would never have to worry about meeting up with the aggressive people, as I do not get involved in conflict, so angry people would not be brought into my life. I do not offer a vibration that would allow this to happen. However, if you have something you wish to be specific about, make sure you are.

You can have control over anything in your life if you want to. If you don't like being stuck in traffic, intend on having a smooth trip as long as possible before you leave and trust it will be. If you don't like queues in shops, then intend otherwise. If you would like a quiet afternoon, plan on having no interruptions and instead peace and quiet.

It is easy to intend anything as long as you let go of the resistance you may have. One year I didn't have plans for Melbourne Cup day and thought I would really like to do something but didn't know anyone who was celebrating. The day after this thought, two of my old work colleagues called out of the blue to say hi, and added, "By the way, we are going to the local hotel for Melbourne Cup day, why don't you come along?"

While I was moving, which can be a most stressful time, I knew to trust and all would be fine, and everything fell together like clockwork. All the disconnections and reconnections happened one after the other and everyone who helped with the move had offered, I did not have to ask a single person for assistance. This is almost a daily occurrence for me, where I simply have a thought and don't have to act on it, as I draw it to me instead of thinking I have to always go in search of it. If I had concerned myself with any of the details regarding the move and started to worry, the help would not have been drawn to me, only difficulties.

If you are always rushing from one place to another, tell yourself you have more time and soon you will. If you want an easier, less frustrating life, intend on it. You will find you will stop misplacing items or locking your keys in your car, getting held up in traffic, whatever it is that is currently causing your life to be chaotic.

Are you currently having a productive
thought or a detrimental one?

Should you happen to get stuck in a queue somewhere, think of intending how the next few hours will be so they will work out in your favor.

If you intend on going on a holiday and want a hassle-free trip, think of it. Don't focus on what could go wrong and expect a smooth sailing holiday. If you intend on a safe journey yet your partner hadn't, you will get a bit of both, unless one has a much stronger intention than the other.

If you want to buy a safe and reliable car, give that your attention. Do not concern yourself with buying a lemon, as that is what you will get. I was looking for a car for my son, and I had to get him to visualize a car that was safe and reliable as well. We only looked at the one car, and the one we bought has been running like a gem ever since. I think it was the best purchase we ever made. Another we wanted to look at that day, the owner was not available. Obviously it was not the right one. However, my sons' previous car had caused us nothing but problems in the beginning. Looking back, that was when I was going through a difficult period in my life where I doubted everything so I got what it was I was offering, although I wasn't aware of it at the time.

If you want your children to be safe, trust they will be; if you worry and believe they are otherwise, that is what you will get. When you become trusting of people and have faith that the universe will only deliver to you someone you can trust, that is what will be. If someone does cross your path with other intentions, you will know instantly by the signs you are being offered. It will be difficult for anyone who is not trustworthy to stay in your life unless you fight it. However, if you are always skeptical of someone's intentions, you will find many people appearing in your life that you have to keep an eye on. The best part of all this, you will find that all the worries that you normally have over these concerns start to disappear, as you can trust you will get what you want. Just make sure if you are asking in accordance with another, that they are intending the same outcome as you.

There might be times when things do happen when you didn't intend them to, as you may be surrounded by many people through work, family, and social outings in big groups or concerts. If you have not made a clear intention before you go (or for some reason you may be feeling anxious, worried and/or flustered), you may wind up with something happening that is out of your control. Even your partner may be thinking differently to you, which would have an influence. You may be in a crowd of people and a fight erupts. If you want to intend safety or any other kind of situation, ask for it clearly as far in advance as you can and focus on it. Let's say you are going to a concert and you want a smooth evening. Focus on that aspect. If the night is not going to go smoothly, you will find it very hard to buy tickets. This is a sign that it is not the night for you to go. Choose another night or miss it altogether. Yet if you are the kind of person who craves excitement and/ or drama, you will be attracting these situations to you and will turn up on a night that a melee will happen.

When I started a job closer to the city working six days a week, I knew that if I did not have a smooth run to work, I would not last too long in the role due my own dislike of having to travel for long periods. I totally trusted that the traffic would be fine driving to work and not once was I ever caught up in it. However, I only set this intention going to work, not coming home; so if at any time I left before 7.00 p.m., the traffic would be chaotic.

I find I always manage to get a parking space when I go out. I visualize it in my mind as I am driving to the destination, and I almost always find it. Why I say 'almost', there has been the odd occasion when I have been annoyed with the traffic along the way—gotten every red light and felt really frustrated. Of course, at those times, I left the house without any clear intentions and got what I was given. Another time, I was driving to the local shops and was having a rare negative thought about a friend; when I got there, to my shock, there wasn't a park. I drove around the block three times only to encounter more frustration. I always understand the reason I get (or don't get) what I want, even if it is not straight away.

Ask for a simpler, easier, stress-free life, and you will find it will come to you. It may take a little while, but you will find things falling into place, and any petty irritations that you usually have will become less frequent.

If you remember one of the earlier stories in the book about the clients who had their home on the market for six months. Had they focused on the home they wanted to move into instead of worrying if their property would sell, I have no doubt they would have attracted a buyer. Instead, they focused on the issue they had with the neighbors', the issue with the stairs and worried that no one would want to buy their home, and that is exactly what happened.

At the time I sold my house I decided I would rent for a while. I viewed a few rental properties and was a little daunted by the renting process. I thought it would be great if I happen to know someone I could rent directly from. I brought home some applications of the properties I viewed and started filling them out. The instant I did my dogs started barking. After I settled them down I went back to filling out the forms, only to be interrupted by a phone call. I decided not to continue with the applications. That very night I was at a house warming party and ran into someone I had not seen in quite a while. They informed me they wanted to rent their house out while they themselves rented a larger house, all coinciding with my own settlement date!

Sometimes you may think that when you want something and it is yet to appear, the universe is telling you that you have to do something else first. For example, maybe you are meant to get the right job before you meet the right partner. That is the case if you believe it. One friend said she wanted to own her own home, which she envisaged to be about five years away before she met her dream man. Once pointed out to her, she thought better to intend differently. These are the kind of thoughts you really need to be clear about when you ask.

22

Life and Other Stories

Your thoughts affect everything that surrounds you, not just your relationships. Your thoughts affect your children, pets, house, your safety, work, car, and your ease of life or your struggles—in fact everything in your life, right down to your telephone bill! If you think life is going to be a hardship, it is. If you start to believe your life is easy, it soon will be.

Take this incident concerning my phone bill; I am sure many people can relate to this. I had an ongoing dispute with my provider and after countless hassles, I decided to change networks. After that I had even more issues with my new provider, so I changed again. Before I was even aware of the power of the mind, I had a friend laugh and tell me that telecommunications and I don't mix. Looking back, I now realize the common denominator was me! I took my negative stance on trying to resolve the issue by changing companies; if only I knew back then not to create a drama and to stop talking to people about the dramas I had, the problem would have sorted itself out. Even now, I can be in the same room with a friend who has the same phone and carrier as I do, and she will have reception when I don't. I gave my old phone from my previous provider to my son who has had no trouble with it, yet I insisted on changing phone companies as I could not get reception!

I knew a person who was always worried that when he leased a property, he would have to move in six months due to the owners no longer wanting him and his family there, for whatever reason. I did not know this person for very long, but in the time I did, I think he had to move three or four times—a case of getting what you don't want when you keep focusing on it.

While in the early stages of writing this book, I wondered if I was capable as I had never written one before, and English being my worst subject at school. However, I asked for help, for my thoughts to be clear and the right words to come to me. In one week I had a constant stream of thoughts that resulted in my putting nearly 60 per cent of this material on pages during that time! The words came to me like a steam train and I started to remember incidents that had been suppressed for years. I had to carry a pen and paper everywhere I went. Another perfect example of the law of attraction bringing one thought after another.

Don't let your today thoughts stand
in the way of your tomorrow.

If you are always frantically backing your computer up as you are worried that one day it will crash, don't worry, it will. Sure, back it up, but don't dwell on the possibility of it happening or you will cause it to.

I have a couple of friends who told me that their life was so good that they were afraid something may happen to put a dampener on that, and sure enough, in time it did. Both have had a few family disasters not long after telling me of their concerns.

A friend who told me a number of times that she hated her job was shocked when she was retrenched. Unfortunately, she did not know that the universe had brought her exactly what she wanted, a reprieve from the job that she hated. She was given the opportunity to find a new job that she would like. It was now up to her to figure out what she wanted to do.

A friend's parents went to the weekly club raffles. They purchased their tickets as usual but did not go with the intention of winning as their fridge had broken down. That night they ended up taking home four meat trays. This is a perfect example of saying no to something, and then having it turning up in like fashion.

In my days of trying to make everything happen, I used to return any missed call on my phone, only to find the calls I did miss were nuisance calls or friends wanting a favor from me at an inconvenient time. I have developed the talent of having people ring me only when I am free and available. I hardly ever receive calls I get 'stuck' in. The phone drops out or something happens to terminate the call. I gladly miss all the calls that are not important at the time.

During my life, I have known some friends of my brothers who seemed to attract the attention of authorities more often than most, even though they knew right from wrong and were good people. They seemed to have a built-in radar letting the law enforcement know of their whereabouts, even when there was no cause for concern. After getting to know them better, the people in question had little respect for anyone who was trying to enforce the law. I now know they were attracting these random events to themselves because of their attitude.

After my divorce settlement in 2005, I was worried about the possibility of my online bank accounts being hacked into and money taken. Several months later my concern became real when a sum of money I had received from the settlement was transferred to an untraceable offshore account.

A while ago I attended a presentation evening where one particular person picked up most of the awards. During a break, almost every conversation was about how they did not think that the person deserved to receive them due to their arrogance and poor sportsmanship. All of the participants, around 900 of them, were then placed in a barrel for the major draw. I could sense everyone in the room hoping the winner of all the awards was not going to win this as well and sure enough, they did! The power of people's collective thoughts pushed this person over the line unintentionally!

I am sure many people have changed providers for many products and services only to end up with the same problems as the last, and we tend to blame the company for bad service. The same often happens with a night out at a restaurant. Don't you find it is always the same people who have issues with the service or their food? It is the one that is always complaining or waiting for something to go wrong, and sure enough, it does. They are either the last to be served or the meal is wrong, cooked incorrectly, or it has a hair in it.

When I ran a cafe at a club a few years back, one particular woman would come in with a group of her friends every month for lunch. Every single time her meal was not what she ordered. Before I knew the laws behind all this, I would cringe every time she came in. I could not believe that the same problem could keep happening to the same person, and I constantly felt irate with the cook, even though it wasn't always the same one working, for not being able to get her order right. This problem happened maybe once a week in general, yet every single time with this particular customer. Her friends started making a joke out of it as she was apparently a compulsive complainer. Now I understand why this was a repeat occurrence. And the reason I was the one always caught in her crossfire was because this was happening at the same time in my life while my sister was dying, my divorce was taking place and various other difficulties were also occurring in my life. I was attracting more difficult situations to myself which would only add to my frustration and anger.

On the same note, while working in furniture retail, I could often determine whether a customer was going to have problems with the purchase of their goods even months prior to their delivery based on the questions they asked and their attitude. Anyone that was demanding or asked questions alleging that the product may be faulty or expected to foresee a problem almost always had an issue.

What we perceive to be 'bad' things generally happen to someone when they are in a negative frame of mind. It is extremely difficult for something 'bad' to happen when you are in a positive frame of mind. However, if you have been giving constant negative attention to something and then decide to change your thoughts, and if you still have the issue in your vibration, it is possible for that concern to still manifest. An example of this is an incident that occurred with my car. For some reason I kept having the thought that something was wrong with it and that I was going to have to spend money; even though when I had bought it, I put out the intention to purchase a safe, reliable, trouble-free car. But my human mind kept telling me otherwise.

After six months of trying to put these thoughts out of my head and in a healthy state otherwise, I caused damage to my car by hitting a pole. The amount of damage I had caused was actually about the amount I had fixed in my mind if I did have a mechanical problem! This story is also a reminder that things do not always happen as intended. Meaning, I thought that the money I would have to spend on the car would be for mechanical reasons. There was nothing mechanically wrong with the car, but because of my worry I drew another kind of worry to me.

Another perfect example of this was an incident my son had while using his bosses work vehicle. His employer reminded him often to be careful driving as any accident he had would be costly as he was a young driver, and the excess was much higher. This concern was even mentioned to me (talking about it always gives it more power). My son was not concerned as he felt he was a competent driver, and had never before had an accident. However, a few months later when he finished an appointment, he walked outside to find the vehicle rolling down the street and slamming into a parked truck. Was the person in possession of the vehicle responsible for the accident or the owner who was putting out the intention (unintentionally) for it to happen in the first place? The incident still did happen while the car was in his care because of the signals the owner was giving out for it to occur, but could not have happened by hitting another vehicle as the drivers thought patterns where not dictating this. So keep in mind things do not always happen as you would think, but they will happen in some way if you give thought to them.

A former work colleague said she was going to give her job two years to take off. Eighteen months later, the job still had not taken off as successfully as she had hoped. Being a firm believer, you get what you ask; she realized what she had asked for and why it was taking so long once it was pointed out. A month later she was topping the sales.

Back in early 2008 my life had become stagnant, I was feeling bored and wanted my life to be a lot more busy. My life certainly became busier but because I was not clear in asking for what it was I wanted, my life turned chaotic over the next few months with countless inconveniences and being involved in friends' dramas. Upon realizing I actually drew these events into my life unintentionally, it wasn't part of a larger plan for me, it was mine, I started to become clearer with my asking. With that I stopped attracting other people's dramas.

This next story doesn't really fit to this chapter however; it follows the last story, due to the chaotic period I created in my life. And had I not been attracting so much drama (unwittingly) into my life at the time, this may not have happened in the first place! I had just moved into my new home and was still unpacking. I got up earlier than usual as I had a large function at work to set up for. I opened the laundry door where my dog Cooper slept to let him out, and he did not follow. Going back in to see why I realized he was gasping for air and I thought that was going to be the end of him! I rang my vet's emergency number however I only got a voicemail. After calling several times, I became frustrated because what was the point of having an emergency number if it is not answered? I was quite panicked, for Cooper and the fact that I knew this was going to set the function right back. I put him in the car and took him to work with me.

Due to Cooper's condition, I parked outside the front of the club, instead of around the back as I normally would so that I could keep an eye on him until the vet called me back. What I had forgotten in my haste was that there was a veterinary clinic a few doors up the road from work which I drove right past since I was going to park out the front. Best of all, they were open at 6.30 on this particular morning for some reason. Had my vet taken my call I would have had to drive 15 kilometers each way in early morning traffic! Not taking my call did me a huge favor, and probably saved Cooper's life. This also demonstrates why things turn out differently even when you can't see it at the time. Having Cooper alive and not inconveniencing hundreds of people were my main priorities.

Life in General

The early stages of this process will be the most challenging for you. This is because your reality is right before your eyes, it is what you are currently living, and more than likely not how you would like your life to be. You need to override the present feelings by looking at how you would like your life to be, not how it is. Now, the hard part is keeping that going when you are constantly looking at what is around you and having everyone pointing out how things currently are. It's hard work to ignore your surroundings, and the changes take time. This is where you need to be mentally strong and persist. Don't let anyone persuade you of otherwise or you will be back to where you started.

While focusing on your destination,
don't forget to enjoy your journey.

Make sure your actions don't contradict your desires. An example of this is based on my own experience. I felt ready to have an intimate relationship again, yet my actions were not warranting that. I quite enjoy my own company and don't like being surrounded by people all the time. I enjoy doing many activities on my own, including things most people like to do with someone else, such as shopping and going to the movies. However, I realized if I didn't change my habits, I would not make room for someone in my life. On the contrary, if you feel needy and need to be in peoples' company all the time, you will either repel the right people for you or attract the wrong ones. There is a very big difference between loving peoples' company and needing people.

Often people are not getting ahead for a few reasons. They are either not thinking of a better life, believing in it, or they're knocking back the opportunities that they have been presented with after they have asked. You still have to make the effort to walk through the doors that open for you. Do not allow your doubt or fear of change or failure to stand in your way. You will only fail if you think you will. People live with regret and the worry of making mistakes. The idea of life is to expand, and with expansion comes challenges and mistakes. Life is all about trial and error. If you do not make mistakes, you are not allowing yourself to expand. Those who used to chastise you as a child when you messed up do not have the control over your life anymore, so release your fear.

Many on a spiritual path often think, "Oh well, I suppose I was just meant to have all this suffering and always be of service to everyone else and remain selfless", but that is not the case. Sure, give and be selfless, if it truly makes you feel good and you don't feel you are missing out. Suffer if you wish, go ahead; you are your own creator. However, don't do it because you feel you have to. Only do it because you want to. Anything you do that is not to your wanting is not for your highest good. And don't feel guilty. You can only help others when you are in a good feeling place yourself, not by begrudgingly doing something you don't want to do. Everyone is here to have their own experience, including those you are assisting.

If you think you have to force something to make it happen, you are having resistance. If you think you have to constantly make phone calls and keep on searching to make it happen, you have resistance. What you want should be easy, and if it's not, it's because it is not the way.

Oftentimes, when you are stuck in a rut and you can't make sense of a situation or how you got yourself there, don't try to analyze it. Your confusion and frustration over your concern will in no way allow you to recognize how it came about, so let it go. Sometime down the track, when the issue has been worked through and dealt with, that is when you will be able to see how you got there in the first place. I am sure you can look back on many situations now and work out your role in it, even though you couldn't at the time. There is always an answer to everything; you just have to find it.

Sometimes, things will not come until you do something else, so let me explain. Let's say you have a desire for a partner and a certain career path. Both are equally important. The career path you desire means a six-month evening course, most nights of the week. Once the course is over, you meet the partner you have always wanted. Why did it happen this way? Because your desire for both was equally strong; if you had met a partner first, chances are you would not have done the course. You would have been too busy spending your nights with your new partner. A six month wait meant you could have both.

I find whenever I hold resistance to anything, my desire does not eventuate, but when I let go, things flow. When people call or text me, I like to get back to them as soon as possible, as I think it is rude not to respond to people. Often people don't have the same courtesy or just don't have the same belief as me, and I find that frustrating; but in my frustration, I don't get a response. I then think after a while, 'My friend has so many kids to look after', or I think that the person is busy, and the next thing, they ring or text back within minutes of me dropping the resistance. The amount of times this has happened, honestly, I couldn't tell you. So just relax into everything; nothing can come while you push against it. Other times plans change; some people drop out from dinner plans or the like, which can be a little irritating. If you focus on the inconvenience, the night will not be as enjoyable; but if you just go with the flow, the perfect people will be there for the topics that are being pondered during the evening.

Once I took a few seconds to look at my life as it was, instead of how I was hoping for it to be, and a sense of dread came over me. I had spent some time off work without pay, and at the time was only in the very early stages of this book, with nothing else to fall back on, or I could face the reality of going back to a line of work that I did not want to do. However, luckily I knew better. Those feelings of dread were overcome quickly, as I knew if that is how I looked at it, then that is how it would be. Instead, I only focused on what I wanted, and then I knew that is what I would get.

The epiphany came when I realized that is how I had always lived my life. When I wasn't happy with how things were; in my fantasizing of how I would like them to be, those thoughts always turned into my reality. Back then, I used to think I was just lucky. Of course, I know now that luck had nothing to do with it. There is no other rational explanation for getting the things I wanted other than I thought them into life.

What I discovered made me realize how people in such horrid circumstances manage to rise above and become successful in their own right. If they had looked at their life as it was, they would never be where they are today. For them to have gotten through such atrocities, they would have to of lived almost all their lives in their head, in their fantasy world. They are more than likely where they are today unintentionally. The reason why, for those as well as me, all those thoughts came to be a reality is because we believed they were only a fantasy, so there was never any attachment to the outcome; they had to happen. That is because the universe cannot distinguish between what you are thinking is real or just a simple thought. It doesn't matter, it will still deliver.

Here is the conclusion I have come to. It doesn't matter if you want it or not. It doesn't matter if it is fantasy or not. If you keep thinking it with the absence of resistance, it has to happen. Here is how resistance works; if you want it and you have resistance to something you desire, it will not turn up. However, if it is something that you don't want and you have resistance or negative emotion surrounding it, it still will. The reason has to do with a universal law. The universe will not deliver to you while you focus on the lack. This is probably life's greatest paradox. You wouldn't want it if you had it, yet focusing on the lack of it will not bring it to you either. That is the reason why those who already have what it is they desire get more and those that don't keep missing out, the rich get richer, the poor get poorer and the gap between the two extremes widens. Once you let go of the feeling of emptiness of not having it, it will be delivered to you as you have detached from the outcome. Clinging to the outcome through acts or thoughts of desperation is the surest way to prevent your desires from coming to fruition.

There are many people who are telling you to live in the present at all costs—telling you to get out of your head and focus on today. Just remember by doing that every single moment means your tomorrow will never get off the ground. Sure, you have to stay in the moment when you are with friends and talking to someone or concentrating on work. Enjoy that cup of tea or food you are eating. But if you want an improved lifestyle, you have to think it into life. It is not going to happen by accident. Does that mean your present does not count? Not at all! Firstly, your present thoughts are the catalyst for your future. You have to find some way of making peace with where you are today for your future to eventuate down the track. Any hostility, anger, or negative emotions need to be let go for an improved future. The more you appreciate your life today, the faster anything you want will come to you.

You won't have to worry about how to make it happen, you will just find that in time life will get better for you and you will be living the life you desire.

24

Staying in Control of Your Life

One problem that we all find really difficult is that we are bombarded with so many different choices to choose from. We tend to feel overwhelmed when we are not up to speed on every conceivable topic. The reason there is so many choices is not for you to know everything, but because we are all very different and unique that if we all wanted the same things, life would be really boring. Many more people are in the world today than ever before, therefore more choices are being made available to accommodate them. This includes the advancement of technology. It is to make way for the increasing population. So first, stop feeling so overwhelmed and just give your attention to what it is you desire and then leave all the rest. The world is full of plenty of things that you both like and dislike. The main aim is to give your attention to what you like and not focus on what you don't. Once you start to do this, you will find that you won't be so bombarded with things that you choose not to have in your life. Your life will stop being as stressful to you if you don't give your attention to issues that you have no direct involvement in.

There is plenty going on in the world, I suggest you focus on the topics that are of interest to you and leave the rest. It is much better to be ignorant and happy than opinionated and out of balance with yourself. Sure, become informed on topics that could affect your life, where you want to have a say on anything that is of interest to you, but if you can't be of any assistance to a topic that is causing you heartache, you are best not worrying about it. If fact, negative thoughts involving any subject can indeed perpetuate the problem at hand by giving more negative energy to the concern. Reading the newspaper and listening to the news are two of the main sources of placing worry in people. Don't you find that as soon as a murder or an earthquake is broadcast, more follow in quick succession? Collective consciousness is gathering and releasing more fear, leading to more of the same. More than 90 per cent of the news reports are on negative subjects, and don't you find it amusing that after twenty-eight minutes of instilling fear in people the program ends with a thirty-second 'feel-good' story?

You do not have to know everything, just the things that are important to you, and then leave all the rest out. The world is full of diverse information so that there is something to intrigue everyone: but you shouldn't feel inadequate at not being informed about every possible topic.

Believe it or not, many people enjoy all the drama they create and actually thrive on it. Fine, just leave them to it; but if it's not for you, stop talking and thinking about things that are of no interest to you and watch how you start to feel more in control of your life.

Why Me?

Everyone has times in their life, some more than others, where they ask 'why me?' They feel like a victim and they spend much time feeling sorry for themselves. It is very hard in times like this to think you bring these circumstances on yourself. There are times when things happen to you, even when you are a child, and you know that you had no control over them and feel so angry and resentful that the situation keeps holding you back. However, you only have two choices: you can continue to dwell in the past and let it keep affecting your life, or you can muster up as much strength as you have and say you are not going to let this beat you anymore and move forward.

I spent much of my time being resentful and holding on to past hurts. But once I knew I was only hurting myself, I had no choice but to change if I wanted a better life. I could keep blaming everyone and everything for what went wrong, or I could fix and change it. Many times I could easily slip back under the dark cloud I had not long ago walked out of. If I spent even a few minutes thinking back to lost opportunities I would be back to square one. It would be so easy for me to do, to look back at the past that was real rather than look to the future I can only visualize and can't see. A few seconds of dwelling and the pain feels like it only happened yesterday. However, I know that if my mind is strong I will reach my next destination.

I spent much time in the past, always looking at the negative aspects of anything. Being a realist, something had to be proved to me before I believed it. It took me a long time to understand that my negative outlook was placing great limitations on my life and preventing my most heartfelt desires from presenting themselves. Once I had reversed this state of mind and saw the possibilities that came with looking at the solutions and wanting resolution, my life took a major turn for the better. The biggest improvement for me came in all my relationships, and my life became so much easier and more stress-free than it ever was. I stopped attracting problems and people who were difficult and negative. I stopped attracting almost all difficult situations. My relationship with my son improved out of sight. Always focusing on him doing well instead of worrying what he was doing wrong made a huge difference. He started to shine. I realized simply by thinking of him so highly helped him reach his potential, all without having to utter more words of encouragement than normal. He could simply pick up on my heartfelt proudness of him.

There is no such thing as a mistake.
It is all life experience.

My constant pushing and trying to make things happen came through years of conditioning by my parents and other influences from as far back as I can remember. I spent many years watching those around me struggle to juggle everything, being angry and resentful most of their lives and placing blame all around them. Their lives appeared to be a constant battle against everything, and I picked up many of their characteristics until I made a conscious effort to change.

There will be times when you really want something and it doesn't happen, but there is always a good reason for this. It is either not what you have been asking for, or there is something better down the track. You cannot see it right now, but in time you will come to realize it. You may have met someone with whom you really wanted a relationship and you were most disappointed when the other person ended it. Then a little while later the perfect partner came along. A partner who had all the qualities you were asking for, not just some. If you had settled for the other one, in time you would have been disappointed and missed out on your dream partner while you were with the wrong one.

You may be very disappointed on missing out on several homes only to find further down the track, your dream home with the pool and double garage you were after at a lesser price. I really wanted to see some great speakers who were holding a seminar in the USA and felt disappointed that I could not come up with the money at the time.

However, instead of spending thousands of dollars on trying to get to a one-day seminar in the United States, I spent a fraction of the cost buying many of their teachings in CD, DVD, and book form, I can now refer to their material time and time again at my leisure. I know there will be many more opportunities in the future to attend their seminars. Know that what you get at the time is more beneficial than it seems.

While having this book written and published there were a few unforeseen hiccups. I could have become frustrated over the hold ups and laid blame (which the old me would have done) however, I knew these incidences were occurring for a reason, even if I did not know what they were at the time. Once I realized my main concern was that of peoples' opinions with regard to some of the radical content in the book and I stopped letting it worry me, everything went according to plan. I worked out that it was my own fear that was holding me back and creating the barriers I was facing.

The universe can't always line things up absolutely perfectly for you, and there will be times when you wouldn't want that to be the case. It can be distressing to want something and have another situation turn out altogether. It is frustrating to be late to work or to an event, yet if you knew that there was going to be a catastrophe at the time you arrived, I am sure you would be happy to have missed it. Sometimes, you are held up because you were meant to run into someone who had an important message you had been wanting an answer to. Other times, it is to keep you safe. If you intended safety over punctuality, then the next two stories will hit home. I am sure all those running late for work on September 11, 2001 were very relieved to be that day as was a friend who was approaching the elevator of the twin towers then realized he left his mobile in his hotel room. A last minute decision to turn back and be late saved his life. Many years ago, a friend and her husband were most distressed when they had missed their flight overseas only to find out that the particular plane they were to travel on had blown open and a number of passengers had plunged to their deaths.

Other times, you will have an intention only to be distracted by something else. More often than not it is for a reason. In the process of completing this book, I intended to be uninterrupted as I was just putting the finishing touches to it and wanted quiet time to do so. No long into it, my son rang asking to be picked up. I told him I wouldn't be long and typed away a little longer. A few minutes later he rang again, wondering where I was and asked me to hurry up. I was quite frustrated with his attitude, insistence and interruptions. I thought to leave, pick him up, and then hurry back to my work. When I walked downstairs towards the kitchen, a candle was well alight and if I had waited any longer, it would have done some serious damage. Of course, I was no longer upset with him once I was aware I had been interrupted for good reason.

Live like you already have it; it will come to you faster.

Another time, when in deep concentration on some work I was doing my computer turned off. I was in a cafe and I knew I had more battery than was I used. I walked back to my car and unknowingly had parked in a one-hour zone. Had I waited any longer, the parking police who were walking towards my car would have issued me a ticket.

Sometimes, there is no good reason as to why you are inconvenienced. I can only surmise that there are millions of people with millions of thoughts for the universe to line up, and they can't all be lined up at the same time. And let's face it, life would be boring if you could predict every single second of every single minute of every single hour of every day. If we did not have some mundane inconveniences at times, it would be hard to appreciate life when everything does go right and falls into place for us to be in awe of.

You may think that you have to suppress normal emotions to get what it is you desire, that you feel that you are not being true to yourself in what you are feeling. I do agree with you. But after a while, I decided that living an existence that I desired overrode the feeling of wanting to justify how I felt all the time. Did I want to continually feel angry, upset, disappointed and sad or be happy and seeing my dreams come to life? The choice is yours; just remember whatever it is you keep thinking will only continue to bring more of the same. I knew more opportunities would be brought to me if I was optimistic as opposed to being pessimistic.

Sometimes, you will have had a situation happen that you feel justified in being angry and telling everyone about the unfortunate and unfair event that occurred to you. Remember, the way you handle the situation and your reaction will determine whether the matter gets sorted out or whether it keeps reappearing in your life. Once you decide to soften your stance, the issue will start to fade. When I broke up with a particular partner, I kept thinking of all the reasons why I did it to justify my guilt; however, this led to me being harassed constantly over our break up. Once I worked out that my thoughts were keeping him bound to me, I released them and let go and the situation stopped.

At times, you will feel that if you just got a break, you would be able to get a handle on it; but unfortunately, we create our own breaks. This can be terribly hard to believe when you are in a situation that is constantly hindering you and everything just keeps on going wrong. I found myself saying many a time, *'there is no way I could have asked for this!'*. It can be very hard to see that when you are smack bang in the middle of it. As I now know better, when I eventually work my way out of a situation, I realize that I did work my way into it as well.

Life is meant to be enjoyed, not be a punishment. We spend so much valuable time going round in circles, making everything so difficult, trying to please everyone else. The most important life to you should be yours. You tend to forget this is your life. If you can't value you, how is anyone else supposed to? Live life how you choose to. Once you start making yourself count, others will too. Others have their own agendas. Let them be their own creator; you just worry about yours. Simply be happy and stop taking everything so seriously. Treat life as a game, especially when things get tough. Try and see yourself from another perspective, outside of yourself. If there are aspects of your life that you love, keep things the same. If there are aspects that you are not happy with, change them. Life is way too long to be spending it not living how you would want it to be, doing the things you love.

There are no hard and fast rules. Stop caring about what everyone else thinks. If that bothers you, don't tell others anything. Once you can get to a point that you don't care about anyone else's opinion, you can tell them whatever you choose to. They have their own life to lead. If the people around you have different wants and desires, love them and let them go to follow their own path. Stop looking back at the past and feeling guilty, resentful or hurt. There is nothing back there that you can change. Just look forward to the future and enjoy it to the fullest.

26

I Am Still Waiting

When things take longer than you would hope, and you are losing a little patience that you start to doubt the concept, especially early in the process, know that is okay; you are human, and until you truly start to believe and see some evidence you will have the occasional slip. Just remember, the powers that be have to move things around to accommodate your request. It is a bit like a game of chess; the universe has to pick people and situations up just like you would a pawn and place them correctly. Some may be a little more stubborn than others, but it will eventually get there. Have your moment of feeling sorry for yourself, blaming everything around you then quickly get over it. It will not serve you if you linger there. It will only hold things away from you that little bit longer. Just remember, it is okay to have moments of not-so-good thoughts. That is only natural. It is also natural to think that you need a break, when you are feeling down that the universe should pick you up and feel sorry for you and make everything okay, but it does not work like that. The most dire countries in the world always have the most natural atrocities. The people who need the help the most have the greatest number of disasters. It is very unfair, but that is how life works; we can't change the rules. You have to go with it if you want to change your life.

At times we can find it difficult to understand or comprehend how an unwanted issue has crept into our lives that would have you wondering, "How and why is this happening?" This can be the most frustrating time in someone's life and be the difference between getting to where it is you want to go and also determining how long it may take for you to get there. Even though it does not feel like it at the time the issue is there for your benefit. Life works in mysterious ways to get you to your desired destination. The hiccup is there to give you a nudge back on track and you may not recognize this instantly, in fact, probably not until you are some distance further down the track and are where it is that you want to be.

So how long should it take for things to change in your life? That depends on a number of factors. Remember, firstly, all the years of thoughts that you have had. Let's say you are forty. Forty years of thoughts have got you to where you are now. Many of those thoughts have still not come to reality yet. The sooner you turn that around in your favor, the sooner things will start to improve. However, remember those thoughts that have not yet materialized; many of them still will. If they were negative, then that is what they will be. They are probably a mixture of both good and ugly.

So start today. You will get what you want sooner, the more you think about what it is you desire. Let's say you get into the habit of thinking about something you want many times during the day. If you can think it ten times a day and it can take hundreds of thoughts to the universe (not adding any counteractive thoughts you may have had), it would turn up in a matter of weeks or months. Keep in mind you have to be a match so some things can turn up in a day, others can take a lot longer. Other times, when you want something and it takes up to six months (or longer), the other person, whoever the universe matches to you has not lined themselves up yet. This is very true of relationships. My girlfriend has met the absolute perfect man for her; however, she did her fair share of waiting. During that time he was leaving a very messy marriage, and it took him a while to get himself back together. Now, they could not be more right for each other. If you asked her if the wait was worth it, there would be no doubt in her reply.

So my answer to that question is, if it is something really big you want, if you keep focusing on it (without resistance), it will probably take six months to a year; relationships could take a little longer, but certainly not always. If it is something smaller, I would say weeks to three months. The time will differ from person to person and situation to situation. You are best to not put a time frame on your desires as that will put strain on the outcome and could hold it away a little longer. Just trust, it will come in good time, when the conditions are perfect. Everything grows in the right conditions. If you think well, the time has been and gone and it is still not here, you have just set it back that little bit more.

You may go for over six months without having any concrete signs in your life, then boom, it happens all at once. This is the universe's way of letting you know that when it brings you three or four things together it is no fluke, it has been prearranged. I will never forget the date of 4 January 2008; I had literally given up, and of course that is when things started to happen, when you let go. I had wanted to stop renting and buy my own home for so long but not being able to sell my investment property that was on the market for 6 months was preventing this. I kept pushing and pushing, trying to make something happen but to no avail. On this date, my son had obtained his driver's license. I was at lunch with a friend telling her how happy I was for him, but the rest of my life had been extremely difficult.

> *Appreciate your life now; it is*
> *your path to your future.*

With that phone rang, and it was the interstate real estate agent appointed to sell my property. They told me they had a buyer who was offering full price for my investment property, which I have never heard of. Next, the another agent rang to say they found a tenant for the property that was vacant for a long time, causing me added financial stress. I was ecstatic and lunch was now going to be a celebration; I told my friend I was going to take my time to buy my own home, that maybe I was trying to rush everything. In that breath, the agent that I was leasing from rang to tell me the house I was renting was going on the market! That was four signs in less than an hour and a half, and after I pondered it a bit more, the area I wanted to buy in was fifteen kilometers away, and my son still had a year of school to go. Looking back, everything was put on hold until he got his license; otherwise, it would have been very difficult trying to get him to and from school. I had also saved a lot of money waiting as the market turned in my favor.

Keep in mind any life changing event that you are just starting to focus on could take a while. The wait will be worth it.

27

A Word of Warning

When you become clearer with your intentions and know what it is that you desire more clearly, you will start to hit a few extra road blocks. This is because you are being more selective, not as many opportunities will be made available to you, the only opportunities will be the ones you want. When you start knocking at the wrong doors, all sorts of barriers will get in the way. This can be most frustrating but remember, it is for your benefit. You want what it is you have asked for; to bring you what it is you want or the closest possible match. It could take a little longer but wouldn't you rather wait a little than rush in, only to then find out it that was not what you wished for? Ride this frustrating time out and you will get your hearts' desires. In fact oftentimes, the universe will slow you down by depleting your energy to stop you making rash decisions and pressing forward when a situation has yet to fully line itself up with you, ensuring you do not take a wrong turn.

Once you have re-conditioned your thinking and your life is going along swimmingly, any small nuances that would not have been a bother to you will actually be a real test when they occasionally arise. You will have gained so much control over your life you will not be used to the odd occasion when you have a slip, something doesn't go according to plan, or other people may also be influencing the environment around you; any hiccup will feel like a major upheaval. Just know that your response will be perfectly normal. You are so used to everything going your way. What's most important is your reaction to the event. If you get worked up over the situation you are only going to attract more of what it is you don't want. Make sure to let go of it as soon as you can to prevent repeat occurrences.

Negative events have a habit of showing up at times sooner than positive events. I can only surmise this happens as negativity seems to have much more power attached than good feelings. For some it is easier to become angry more quickly than it is to get into a happy state. So make yourself aware of this.

An example is the following story of my own. A while back I received an invoice for double the amount it should have been. Weeks later and still no resolution, only a threatening letter of demand, I kept dwelling on how the problem hadn't been resolved and the frustration surrounding it. Then a barrage of negative thoughts overtook me. People I had left messages with who had not returned my calls and others that had let me down; now I was on an attack! Here I was, someone trying to show others how to take control of their lives through their thoughts and I was feeling at my wits' end! Then it dawned on me, what was the outcome I was hoping to achieve? For the bill to be rectified so I could pay it! So instead of focusing on why it was not fixed, I immediately thought of the outcome I desired.

Within a minute my frustration turned to hope. It can be surprising how quickly you can change your emotions so dramatically just by changing your thoughts. I quickly dropped the resistance I had surrounding this issue, and a few hours later, the problem was resolved. I asked myself, 'Why had I not done this weeks ago?' The answer is because I am human, and our emotions get in the way. I also realized it had dragged on so long because every time I opened the mail I expected to see the double payment, not the situation rectified.

See how we bring these kinds of problems on ourselves? Wayne Dyer, author of *Real Magic*, wrote in the Foreword of Jerry and Esther Hicks' book Ask *And It Is Given*, "When you change the way you look at things, the things you look at change." How very true!

28

Some Last Tips

I f you think there is not enough, there won't be. If you think there is plenty, then there will be. The choice is yours. Do you want to live in fear or hope, in lack or abundance? Do you see your glass as half-full or half-empty? Stop being anti anything and be pro everything. The media tends to surround us with fear. Mostly what we see on our news is fear based as well as many programs which are supposed to be informative. It is almost always the negative aspects of a subject. That is because people tend to focus on drama. Most love the drama. Who is getting blown up, who is dying, what is the new disease that is appearing, what animals are becoming endangered. By trying to make us aware, we are adding negative influence to these problems thereby making them worse, not better.

Instead of focusing on what is going wrong, focus on how to right it. Be solution-oriented instead of problematic. It does not help to be informed on any subject if it is going to activate a negative vibration in you or around the situation involved. You are much better off not knowing or being informed if that is the case. If you want to be informed great, but don't become inundated, feeling good should be your main concern. There is way too much going on in the world to have an opinion on everything. If you cannot be of positive assistance, what is the point of knowing? It would be best to only stick to topics you are passionate about and can assist, then leave the rest.

Do not think about any future events that you do not want. *Anything.* Do not think of sickness, being broke, being stuck in traffic, the car breaking down, being without money, getting retrenched, one of the kids having an accident, wondering what will happen to your parents as they age. It doesn't matter what the thought is, any negative aspect you give too much attention to will eventually manifest. Worrying about anything is like a rocking chair; you keep going backwards and forwards but you aren't getting anywhere. If something does happen that you don't wish for again, stop the worry. Worry will not fix it or make it go away. Worry will keep you from the solution to fixing the problem. A problem can only ever be solved when you are looking for a solution. Whenever you have an issue that you feel you cannot solve due to the frenzy surrounding it, ask to have someone brought to you who will help solve it for you or with you. That person will appear when the time is right to fix the problem.

Turn every negative into a positive;
every problem into a solution.

In Closing

have endless stories I could keep adding but why, when you would have so many of your own. If you took the time to think about them, you would realize they didn't all happen by chance. Take stock of your own life.

Don't let everyday life weigh you down and stifle your dreams. Do what is meaningful to you. I couldn't imagine anything worse than lying on your death bed with regrets because of what you should or should not have done. Don't let that happen to you. Your life counts.

Since I have discovered this magic, I do not let any minor irritations bother me anymore. Things that I would once worry about are now like water off a ducks back. I hardly bother with the newspaper and keeping abreast of the latest current affairs, hearing depressing news about people dying and other major catastrophes happening around the world, or issues with the government or the environment. That doesn't mean that I don't care, I just now know that my worry doesn't do any good and in fact hinders my own life and those that I am helping. If I can help by offering assistance or making a donation, I will; other than that I will not give my attention to anything that I do not have any control of as my grief will make the matter worse. I do my bit and trust everyone will do theirs. I would much rather be happy and healthy than informed and troubled. The same goes with my close friends and family. Do I still have compassion? Yes, I do. But I will not wallow in anyone's self-pity as I know they have the ability to make things better for themselves if they choose to. They only have to ask to hear the answer.

I am aware that anything which shows up in my life, I have somehow allowed it in by giving it my attention, so I no longer blame others when things go a little awry, which is not very often at all. Just like publishing this book. I never doubted for a minute that the right person would come along and help this book reach the many targeted readers it was intended for.

My biggest comfort comes from knowing that I do not have to fear anything as nothing can harm me if I never offer enough negativity to it. That is my greatest feat. The old me would try and control all of my surroundings with my actions. Now I know if I let go and think my way through the processes, I trust the right situations will come to me. I do not have to make the agonizing choices that I used to and then wonder if I went the right way.

Still skeptical, I totally understand. If you are anything like me, you will need to have a mountain of proof. That's fine. Just put it all to a test yourself however, be careful not to be too critical; your doubt will stop the allowing of wonderful synchronicities happening. Just always remember to *Think Before You Think*. Nothing teaches more than your own life experiences; for you have to form your own beliefs and opinions. However, I trust my words do stimulate your thoughts. This book is based on my experiences, and I wanted to share with you some principles and techniques I have learnt to make my life easier. You may be a little skeptical when you start, but once you start seeing the benefits for yourself, your beliefs will change. Even if you only take on one aspect of these principles and integrate it into your life for a more rewarding future, it has been of benefit to you.

Once you get on your way you will start to build momentum. Magical things will start to happen. There are no mistakes. It is all part of the grand design. I am always amazed with every little sign I get. It feels like I have a direct link to the universe that I can access at any time, which is exactly what it is. You can too.

You may have heard the same message several times throughout this book. That is just to make sure you understand the importance *of understanding the importance of it*. I know when I hear the same message over and over, it ingrains deep within me so I not only remember, but helps to buoy my faith.

*You mind is magnetic. Are you going
to attract or repel your desires?*

Is my life perfect and always on track? Far from it! Just because I know these principles doesn't mean I'm always in tune and apply them. At times I still grow impatient with the waiting it takes and forget to enjoy the moment, something I think I will need to practice forever.

When you feel bored, restless, and unfulfilled, do not be concerned. It means that you have a need to expand and are seeking more in your life. So go on the journey of determining what it is that you are yearning for that would make you feel fulfilled. Once you find it, you will be satisfied for a period of time, although I am not sure how long. Then you may want to expand again. Life is a never-ending journey of seeking fulfillment. If you did not keep having new desires, you may as well be dead. Look at Richard Branson, a man who has anything and everything that he could hope for. That does not stop him from coming up with new ideas and looking for more. So don't feel guilty for always wanting more; there would be no reason to be living if you stopped desiring.

Your action is the result of your previous inner thoughts; meaning, you live your life from the inside out, not the other way around. Let go of your worry and trust in your inner being that is guiding you.

We apparently have thousands and thousands of thoughts a day. I want you to give thought to your thoughts. How much of that time would you spend in appreciation or focused on the how you want your life to be? Include all your thinking time, when your mind wanders while working, or engaged in a task that needs your concentration—times in the car, on the bus, mowing the lawn, doing the cleaning. When you manage to increase that substantially, things will start working much more smoothly for you.

You are probably wondering why this book is so short. Because it really is simple; what needs to be said has already been stated. I could make it longer or draw it out, but why? Just to confuse you and make it more than it is? The whole idea is to simplify your life, not make it more difficult. How simple is it to start focusing on exactly what it is you want, take your attention off what it is you don't; enjoy the journey while you are waiting and trust you will get exactly that? Think about what you want and nothing else. Live it, breathe it, feel it. It is that easy.

Once you start 'wondering where is it?, what if you have asked wrongly, you don't deserve it; well presto, your wish is the universe's command. Just trust, totally trust. Be your own genie. The universe will bring it to you in such a way you will know you are heading in the right direction. You will not miss any signs, for they will be loud and clear to you. You have nothing to lose by having faith and believing, apart from your happiness. And once you have found it, spread the word.

One Last Word

Just as important, if not more so, is to think before you act. Sometimes, your actions and your words can be very harmful to others as well as yourself. Thoughts can be changed before they have an impact, actions and words cannot. Before you do anything that could be damaging, think about the consequences of your actions, whether this entails revenge, doing something destructive to yourself, getting behind the wheel while you are drunk or saying or doing something that might be harmful to someone else, especially if it is a loved one. They may be able to forgive you, but not necessarily forget, and it may drive you from their life for good. Ask yourself if that is what you want? Your actions or words cannot be reversed, so before you go ahead, will what you have to do or say be of benefit to you or someone else? In the words of Neale Donald Walsch, "What would love do now?"

The End

Important Note

This book is in no way intended to replace medical or psychological help.

Please seek any medical assistance needed should you feel that treatment be required.

Think Before You Think is based on the authors own experiences and opinions. Those wishing to use any information pertained in the book for their own benefit do so at their own risk and using their own judgment.

Notes

Notes

Notes

Notes

Notes

Notes

Notes

Notes

Notes

Notes

Printed in the United States
By Bookmasters